0061972

W9-BKK-419

3 1702 00096 9463

DATE DUE

MAR. 2 2 1993	
APR. 1 8 1994	
APR 1 8 1996	
DEC 0 2 1997	

HOW TO GET

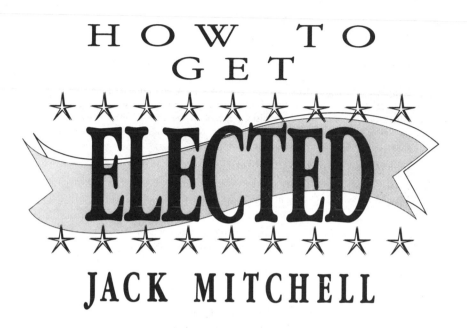

ELECTED

JACK MITCHELL

AN ANECDOTAL HISTORY
OF MUDSLINGING, RED-BAITING,
VOTE-STEALING, AND DIRTY TRICKS
IN AMERICAN POLITICS

ST. MARTIN'S PRESS   NEW YORK

Design by Judith Christensen

Library of Congress Cataloging-in-Publication Data

Mitchell, Jack
    How to get elected : an anecdotal history of mud-slinging, red-baiting, vote-stealing, and dirty tricks in American   politics /
Jack Mitchell.
        p.   cm.
    Includes index.
    ISBN 0-312-07794-7
    1. Political corruption—United States—History.   2. Elections—United States—Corrupt practices—History.   I. Title.
JK2249.M58   1992
324.7'0973—dc20   92-2680
                                                                CIP

First edition: July 1992

10   9   8   7   6   5   4   3   2   1

ACKNOWLEDGMENTS

First, I'd like to thank my good friends and colleagues, Joe and Susan Trento, for their invaluable assistance and encouragement in this most enjoyable project; it would not have been initiated without their participation. Second, I'm grateful for the generous contributions of many friends and colleagues in the journalistic and political worlds who are too numerous to list by name here (some would prefer not to be identified in any event, I'm sure). Particular thanks to the capable staffs of the Library of Congress's prints and photographs division and the Smithsonian Institution's political history office are in order for their helpful role in assisting my illustrations research.

Finally, I'm especially appreciative of the expert and gentle guiding hand of my editor, Bill Thomas. His organizational ideas, refinements, and patient supervision shaped this work to a great degree. Knowledgeable editors remain a critical part of any book-writing process; that fact is clearly evident in these pages.

FOR MY LOVING PARENTS,
JACK F. AND JANE S. MITCHELL

CONTENTS

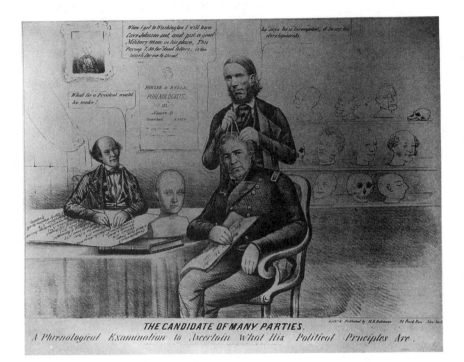

THE CANDIDATE OF MANY PARTIES.
A Phrenological Examination to Ascertain What His Political Principles Are.

ILLUSTRATIONS

Illustration acknowledgments: p. ii reproduced with permission from The Henry E. Huntington Library and Art Gallery, San Marino, California; pp. x, xvi, 21, 50, 68, 74, 84, 98, 108, 121, 124, 154, 174, 182, 192 Smithsonian Institution; pp. 11, 31, 42, 60, 91, 115, 128, 138, 147, 162 Collections of the Library of Congress.

INTRODUCTION

In today's world of instantaneous communication—chock-full of repetitive, opinion-shaping, often confusing images—the impression left for many American voters is that present-day politics has become the vilest, dirtiest, most reprehensible tool of democratic government. Certainly, there's considerable empirical evidence to support that point of view, a good deal of which is detailed in these pages.

Yes, politics can be and often is a nasty business: but that's nothing new on the American election scene. George Washington was ferociously attacked and shamelessly ridiculed to an extent unimagined by his modern successors in the White House. In fact, the constant haranguings the Founding Father took from the ink-stained wretches of the late eighteenth-century press ultimately influenced his decision to retire from public life.

It's difficult to imagine any candidate of recent times successfully surviving revelations that he had fathered an illegitimate child and still being elected president of the United States, as Grover Cleveland was in 1884. Juicy, often unprovable allegations against candidates concerning sexual misbehavior, fondness for the bottle, or financial chicanery aren't a product of the electronic age. On the contrary, candidates of the 1990s who complain about being unfairly vilified by their opponents and the paid image-makers of television-dominated campaigns must be blissfully unaware of the no-holds-barred elections of the past. Much of what is regarded as outrageous now is tame compared to the character-destroying election warfare of earlier generations.

For example, it's incorrect to assume that the "Willie Horton-izing" of Democratic presidential hopeful Michael Dukakis during the White House election race of 1988 was the worst savaging of a candidate for national office, as some observers have asserted. Indeed, as you'll see in *How to Get Elected*, there's evidence that the Massachusetts governor's campaign ads were as negative as George Bush's. The critical difference was that the Democrats' ripostes just weren't as *effective* as the Republican-crafted media spots in swaying voter opinion.

Mudslinging, name-calling, negative campaigning—by any name, the underhanded politics of rumor, gossip, and innuendo have been an intrinsic, if frequently unpleasant, part of the American election experience at every level. Occasionally the broadsides have been amusing and informative; more often, the personal assaults have been ugly, divisive, and brutal. Perhaps most significantly, the head-hunting, knife-in-the-back tactics have been dragged out, dressed up, and repeated in various forms decade after decade for a simple, time-tested reason. *They work.*

Picking up the political rock and examining its slimy, crawly underside, however, is essential to an understanding of the crazy quilt that makes up the American electoral process; and it's necessary, in this writer's opinion, if any meaningful change or reform is to occur. Voters may take heart: we've always thought our would-be political saviors had feet of clay. And more often than not, the critics have been proven right. Keep in mind, though, that as usual in the democratic system, the stumbling and bumbling often looks and sounds far worse than the final result.

The collection of anecdotes, stories, and sayings that follow aren't intended to encourage the cruel purveyors of the smear and "Big Lie" techniques familiar to the politics of hate. Rather, they're meant as a modest guideline, to help the reader visualize the impressive heights to which American campaigns, elections, and their participants could soar by recognizing the agonizing depths to which they've often sunk. Enjoy.

Some Account of some of the Bloody Deeds of
GEN. JACKSON.

| Jacob Webb. | David Morrow. | John Harris. | Henry Lewis. | David Hunt. | Edward Lindsey. |

Gen. Jackson, detailing his progress among the Indians.

FRANKLIN, Tenn. September 10, 1828.

THOMAS HART BENTON, Lieut. Col. Thirty-Ninth Infantry.
And now a member of the Senate of the United States.

SLANDER, LIES, AND MUDSLINGING

THE MEDIA'S "WHIPPING BOY"

Almost every president has complained about what he regarded as unfair and unflattering coverage by the media. But the modern chief executives had it easy compared to George Washington, who decided not to run for a third term as president partially because of the bashing he was taking in the freewheeling press of the late eighteenth century. "A disinclination to be longer buffeted in the public prints by a set of infamous scribblers" was how Washington described his decision to opt for retirement from public life.

"Probably no man in American history suffered more than Washington from newspaper libels, from a reviving of old lies and the concoction of new ones with a wild irresponsibility that American mores would not accept today," noted historian James Thomas Flexner.

In 1793, a New York journal carried unsubstantiated assertions that "aristocratical blood" flowed in Washington's veins, and that "gambling, reveling, horseracing and horse whipping" had been cornerstones of his education, according to an account by lawyer Joseph Cooper. In private business, he was a "most horrid swearer and blasphemer," despite his religious pretentions.

The first president was unpopular with anti-Federalist writers all up and down the East Coast of the United States. In New Jersey, the opposition press compared him to a "king," and a Philadelphia paper claimed he had been flattered by the "opiate of sycophancy" into becoming an arbitrary, power-hungry leader. Another paper mocked him as "Saint Washington"; and he was damned by one exaggerating critic as the "debaucher of a nation," a comment that would undoubtedly result in a million-dollar libel suit today.

Washington did complain about the printed assaults against him—but privately. "To persevere in one's duty and be silent, is the best answer to calumny," he wrote. The press's piling on, however, finally soured him on remaining in elective office, where he'd served since the age of 26.

WE'RE PRETTY DISGUSTED TOO, ABBY

A host of long-festering political scores were settled during the presidential election campaign of 1800; some of the wild, round-house blows landed by the feuding candidates and their supporters would make even the toughest of today's image-makers cringe. No one was spared.

President John Adams, running with the Federalist party, was hopeful of reelection, despite a first term plagued with a foreign scandal commonly called the XYZ affair, in which French agents tried to bribe American diplomats. He also suffered from the disloyalty of key advisers, and the behavioral problems of a rather troubled family, whose drinking, health, and other woes would have broken a lesser man. Although his origins were lower-middle class, Adams was branded as an aristocrat and monarchist. Phony stories were conjured up that he was plotting to marry one of his sons to a daughter of King George III and produce some sort of transatlantic ruling dynasty.

It's a myth that the Founding Fathers all got along like close-knit pals during the first generation of our nation's democratic government. On the contrary, many of the fledgling country's leading citizens openly detested each other: Adams, for instance, referred to the prominent Alexander Hamilton as "the bastard brat of a Scotch pedlar," not totally without cause. Hamilton had published a pamphlet, later widely circulated by Adams's opponents, accusing him of vanity, extreme egotism, and generally reckless behavior in office.

The Adams haters, and there were many, also attacked his vice-presidential running mate, Charles Cotesworth Pinckney (the hero of the XYZ affair for having turned down a proffered bribe with the retort "not a sixpence"). Pinckney supposedly had been sent to England to "procure four pretty girls as mistresses, a pair for each elderly gentleman." This tavern gossip amused more than outraged Adams, who replied in a letter to a friend that "I do declare upon my honor, if this be true, General Pinckney has kept them all for himself and cheated me out of my two."

The Federalists' backers also got in their digs, however. Adams's Democratic-Republican opponent, Thomas Jefferson, was accused of being a plagiarist, and having adopted the Declaration of Independence from the writings of the English philosopher John Locke. He was also charged with not believing in God and being an "infidel," untrue allegations to which he initially refused to respond out of principle; but the rumors alone caused some devout Federalist women to wonder where they should hide their Bibles if Jefferson won the election.

One critic, Cotton Mather Smith, claimed Jefferson had amassed personal wealth from the estate of a widow whose properties he had administered. A vituperative Federalist described Jefferson as a "mean-spirited, low-lived fellow, the son of a half-breed Indian squaw, sired by a Virginia mulatto father. . . ."

The actual vote was just the beginning of Jefferson's woes; he narrowly won more electoral ballots than Adams, but tied with his Republican running mate, Aaron Burr, with seventy-three votes each. In those days that meant the House of Representatives would have to break the deadlock, for while everyone knew Jefferson had been running for the top spot, it wasn't automatically his unless Burr conceded it to him, which he declined to do when he saw the possibility of running the show himself.

Ironically, many Federalist legislators preferred Burr to Jefferson and were prepared to vote that way until Hamilton, who apparently had enough bile in him to spew at an army of enemies, decided he hated Burr even more than Jefferson and intervened to keep Burr from winning an unexpected victory.

After that ordeal, which resulted in his becoming America's third president in what he hyperbolically called "the revolution of 1800," Jefferson should rightly have been expecting a little respect. No such luck. His ascension to power caused his critics to turn up the volume with even uglier rumors about the new chief executive. Anti-Republican journalists wrote that he had been a libertine since his college days, and that he'd tried to seduce the wife of a classmate. He was also accused of initiating affairs with two matrons while serving in Paris, and of fathering several children by a black slave named Sally Hemings at his

Monticello estate (which, unlike the other allegations, appears to have been true).

The outgoing president's wife, Abigail Adams, summed it up pretty well when she asserted that she had "heard so many lies and falsehoods propagated to answer electioneering purposes that I am disgusted with the world."

THE IVY WALLS OF ACADEME

While it's probably true that Thomas Jefferson had what could be regarded as a somewhat liberal attitude toward relations with women, given his celebrated liaison with one of his female slaves, he undoubtedly wasn't expecting the kind of withering campaign blast he received in 1804 from the president of Yale University. The reelection of Jefferson, charged Timothy Dwight, "would make our wives and daughters the victims of legalized prostitution."

President Jefferson was returned to office without the support of the blunt-spoken college administrator. History does not record any sudden upsurge in prostitution during Jefferson's second term.

THOSE VILE WRETCHES

Divorce was used as a presidential campaign issue long before it hampered Nelson Rockefeller's chances to live in the White House.

With the help of his own immense personal popularity and a boost from a well-established party organization years in the making, Andrew Jackson—the spike-haired, formidable "Old Hero" from Tennessee—won the presidential election of 1828. But even as he was inaugurated in a riotous affair featuring drunken fistfights and window smashing, the depressed, ill General Jackson believed his beloved wife Rachel's premature death just three months before had been at least partially caused by the campaign slanders of his political enemies.

A simple woman who never wanted to leave her beloved Hermitage estate for "that palace in Washington," Rachel Jackson became the target of gossip for anti-Jackson campaign operatives who knew her husband was impervious to any sort of insult. (Not that they didn't try—he was called a mulatto, a butcherous military commander, a gambler, and a home wrecker.)

Mrs. Jackson was labeled an adulterer because her unstable, insanely jealous first husband, Captain Lewis Robards, lied when he wrote that he'd granted her a divorce long after their separation. For years afterward, armed with pistols and his famous hickory cane, Jackson fought duels of honor to defend his beloved wife's reputation; one such confrontation resulted in an embedded bullet that remained in Jackson's body for the rest of his life.

His ornery habit of shooting his wife's critics didn't stop Jackson's many detractors, who were determined to block his ascent to the White House, from leveling charges of bigamy against him. "The enemys of the Gel's have dipped their arrows in wormwood and gall and sped them at me," Rachel wrote to a friend.

When she died a month after an election that should have been Jackson's greatest moment of triumph, the Old Hero was inconsolable. At her graveside during the Christmas season of 1828, Jackson proclaimed bitterly: "In the presence of this dear saint I can and do forgive all my enemies. But those vile wretches who have slandered her must look to God for mercy."

THE LITTLE MAGICIAN

Martin Van Buren got an unwelcome dose of the nasty politics of the personal in 1836, when his Democratic party's opponents made the personality and style of the adroit little politician the central issue of the presidential election. His detractors attempted to wreck Van Buren's image long before the campaign began, portraying the red-whiskered politician as the sly, cunning "Red Fox." Although his diminutive physical stature and considerable skills had earned Van Buren the nickname the "Little Magician," critics turned it against him by labeling him as an unprincipled, scheming intriguer. He was a "master hand at trippin folks who stand in his way," according to one satirical account of the time, which also described Van Buren as a man who buttered his bread on "both sides at once."

In an effort to counter the heroic popularity of Van Buren's mentor, the legendary military hero Andrew Jackson, the Whigs recruited the famous frontiersman Davy Crockett to lend his name to a scurrilous, ghostwritten biography of Van Buren, which claimed that he was nothing more than a self-serving professional politician. Van Buren regarded public office, not as a service, but he "pushed it as a trade," stated the polemic, which was published before Crockett's death at the Battle of the Alamo in 1836.

Other broadsides described Van Buren as a "third rate man" who was skilled at "gittin all his folks into office," while his political colleagues were a "knot of cat-paced, sly-faced, cringing, artful, busy fellows."

That was the tame stuff, according to Van Buren biographer Donald Cole. The Whigs also savagely attacked Van Buren's personal appearance, making him out to be little more than a dandified fop. One writer of the day described Van Buren as "tastily and even dantily dressed," and other taunts suggested that it was difficult to distinguish with his "delicate slipper(s) . . . whether he was man or woman."

The Little Magician had the last laugh, however. He won a close election and sent the Whigs home crying.

ARSENIC AND OLD ZACH

Although he'd never voted in a presidential election, knew next to nothing about the issues, and professed to have little interest in being a candidate, General Zachary Taylor, Louisiana's "Old Rough and Ready," was the Whig party's standard-bearer in 1848. The Whig bosses wanted a winner, not the best-qualified candidate, and that's what they got. A genuine military hero was worth ten political hacks.

The Democrats, who'd nominated Michigan's rotund Senator Lewis Cass, greeted General Taylor with a salvo of campaign epithets designed to knock down his reputation a peg or two. He was compared to Caesar and Napoleon, accused of being a military dictator, semiliterate, a cruel slavemaster, and a slob (the last charge having more than a ring of truth—the rumpled Taylor was no Beau Brummel).

More accustomed to praise for his considerable military accomplishments, Taylor took the personal attacks, well, personally—he said the campaign was marked by "the vilest slanders of the most unprincipled demagogues this or any other nation was ever cursed with, who have pursued me like bloodhounds."

His partisans didn't just sit back and take the abuse. The Whigs portrayed Cass as a windbag ("General Gass"), which was probably the nicest thing they said about the senator. He was also branded a slave trader, a graft taker, and a real estate speculator.

Taylor survived the verbal slugfest and won the election, partially because former president Martin Van Buren split the vote with the Free-Soil party; in addition, Senator Cass wasn't exactly beloved within his own party. As president, Taylor showed himself to be a bit more broad-minded than he'd been given credit for earlier, and led an effort to prohibit the expansion of slavery, though he wasn't personally opposed to it.

In July 1850, however, Taylor contracted what was probably acute gastroenteritis from bolting down a large amount of cherries and cold milk soon after a long walk in the stifling heat of Washington. His doctor's blundering ministrations probably helped kill him. Even then poor Old Rough and Ready wasn't allowed to rest in his grave. Clara Rising, a historian who theorized that Taylor had been poisoned by political rivals opposed to his actions on slavery, convinced officials to exhume the 140-year-old corpse from its tomb in Louisville, Kentucky, to test for signs of arsenic. They found none.

PILLORYING "THE PATHFINDER"

A man of principle, the storied explorer John Charles Frémont turned down feelers by the Democrats to head their presidential ticket in 1856 because the party supported slavery. Rebuffed, they turned to Pennsylvanian James Buchanan. Frémont might later have wished he'd stayed out of politics altogether when the newly formed Republican party, whose opposition to slavery was one of its primary tenets, convinced him to lead their campaign instead. With the inclusion of Whig candidate Millard Fillmore and his xenophobic Know-Nothing party, which was mainly in existence to attack Catholics and immigrants, the race was tough, close—and dirty.

Delighted to have a heroic public figure as their standard-bearer, the Republicans did all they could to build up the legend of the famous "Pathfinder," one of the greatest excursionists in American history. Meanwhile, his opponents ganged up on the adventurer, who wasn't much of a politician in any event. First the Know-Nothings, living up to their name, assailed Frémont for being a Catholic, although he quickly proved he was an Episcopalian, noted biographer Ferol Egan. But his father had been a Catholic and Frémont and his wife Jessie had been married by a Catholic priest, and that was enough for the hate-mongers.

Then the frontiersman suffered the indignity of his illegitimate birth becoming a public issue. Frémont also was accused of being falsely credited with discoveries he'd never claimed, of being a hard drinker, a brutalizer, a secret slaveholder, and a financial cheat. Southern businessmen were warned Frémont's election might ruin the slave-based economy of that region; the anti-Frémont slurs culminated in the ugly campaign slogan "Free soilers, Fremonters, free niggers, and freebooters."

The three-ticket split cost Frémont votes, as did the absence of support from the powerful former senator Thomas Hart Benton, his father-in-law, who couldn't support a non-Democrat for president, even if he was a member of the family.

Despite the fusillade of intensely personal slander, Frémont did well at the polls; he came in a respectable second to Buchanan in a vote where third-place spelled the end of the line for the Whig party.

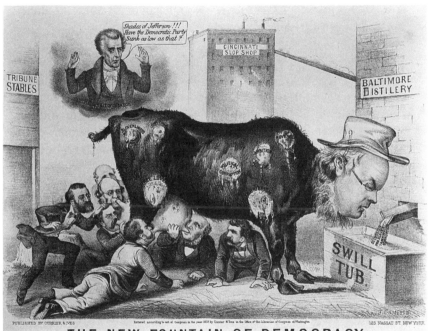

THE NEW FOUNTAIN OF DEMOCRACY,
Swill Milk for Hungry Suckers.

LITTLE STEVIE'S LOST

With today's presidential hopefuls invading the living rooms of early-primary state voters in Iowa and New Hampshire a full eighteen months before the election, it's hard to believe that at one time, hitting the campaign stump was considered a degrading practice for a candidate. For example, Stephen Douglas, the oratorically brilliant "Little Giant" who debated Abraham Lincoln in 1860's presidential sweepstakes, was sharply criticized for making dozens of stump speeches on the campaign trail.

"It is not a seemly or a welcome sight to see any man whom a large portion of his countrymen have thought fit for the Presidency, transversing the country and soliciting his election thereto," declaimed one offended observer. Douglas made a clumsy attempt to hide the true purpose of his travel schedule by announcing he was visiting his mother, who told one interviewer that she expected her son daily, but that "he never writes when we may expect him."

The transparent excuse brought ridicule from one editor, according to Douglas biographer Robert Johannsen. Describing Douglas's supposed "maternal pilgrimage," a leaflet was circulated, asking for information on the " 'BOY' LOST." He "Left Washington, D.C. some time in July, to go home to his mother, in New York . . . He is about five feet nothing in height, and about the same diameter the other way. He has a red face, short legs and a large belly. Answers to the name of 'Little Giant.' Talks a great deal, and very loud; always about himself. He has an idea that he is a candidate for the Presidency. Had on, when he left, drab pants, a white vest, and blue coat with brass buttons; the tail is very near the ground."

LAMBASTING THE LINCOLNS

Voters who think modern-day campaigns are vicious and unfair should have been around for the 1864 presidential election. Abraham Lincoln is revered today as one of the greatest chief executives in American history. He was in the midst of bravely guiding his country through the most divisive crisis in its history when he sought reelection in the waning months of the Civil War. One would think the besieged President Abe would have gotten some political slack simply for gamely trying to cope with the wrenching enormity of the nation's travails. Wrong. His legion of detractors unleashed an unprecedented campaign of invective designed to remove him from the White House.

Not that Lincoln wasn't used to name-calling. "Ape . . . gorilla . . . monster . . . mulatto . . . a rawboned, shamble-gaited, bow-legged, knock-kneed, pigeon-toed, slob-sided, shapeless skeleton in a very tough, very dirty, unwholesome skin" were just some of the phrases that greeted his election and inauguration in the spring of 1861. The intervening three or four years hadn't taught his critics any manners.

The Democrats' candidate, Union General George McClellan, was called a "cowardly traitor" by the Republican press, and was denounced as a turncoat who would sell out the blue-coated forces for politically favorable peace terms. Not to be outdone, Lincoln haters in the North were openly discussing his assassination. Incredibly, one Democratic newspaper in Wisconsin editorialized: "If he is elected to misgovern for another four years, we trust some bold hand will pierce his heart with dagger point for the public good."

Nor were the campaign epithets hurled only at the sad-eyed, brooding leader. His family also became a target for Lincoln's political enemies. The temperamental Mary Lincoln, already a nervous wreck because of the loss of her son Willie to typhoid fever in 1862, drew unmerciful fire from all angles. She was accused of being a spendthrift, a "coarse, vain, unamiable woman," with "no conception of dignity" who refused to pay her bills and dressed outlandishly and unsuitably for a First Lady. Earlier, she'd been criticized for trying to keep her eldest son Robert out of the army, whispers that ceased only when her husband found a place for the young Harvard graduate on the staff of General U. S. Grant.

Lincoln's electoral victory in November 1864 brightened her spirits, but her joy over her spouse's political vindication and the collapse of the Confederacy were to be cut short within months by the actor John Wilkes Booth and his fellow conspirators.

MAKE ROOM FOR DADDY

A favorite theme of presidential politics in the eighteenth and nineteenth centuries was illegitimate children and the politicians who allegedly fathered them. Thomas Jefferson was one such target of whispers that he'd sired children by a black slave (the allegations were possibly, even probably true, depending upon which historian's version of events you accept). Grover Cleveland was another candidate accused of fathering a bastard child (maybe guilty; and to his credit, he freely admitted his earlier relationship with the mother and agreed to support the out-of-marriage offspring).

The topic also arose in the presidential election of 1868, when the Democrats had to create something to counter the unchallenged heroic profile of the Republicans' incumbent candidate and Civil War hero, Ulysses S. Grant. On this occasion, according to one Grant biographer, the general was accused of having fathered an Indian daughter in Vancouver. The campaign whispers lost credence, though, when it was determined that the child in question had been born less than nine months before Grant's arrival in the area. The real father was more likely a "Richard" Grant.

Neither that nor the repeated tales of Grant's habitual drunkenness stopped the once-failed shopkeeper from Galena, Illinois, from defeating the now-forgotten Democrat, Horatio Seymour.

329

During the presidential election of 1880, the number "329" was scrawled on many fenceposts and billboards across America. The three digits were an effective campaign slogan against the Republican candidate, James Garfield. Years before, while serving in Congress, the Ohio-born General Garfield had been caught up in what was known as the Credit Mobilièr scandal.

When the Tammany-backed Smith took office in early 1919, Hearst's hard-charging news organization accorded the new governor a honeymoon of sorts. Within a few months, however, perhaps because Hearst felt the popular Smith represented a threat to his own presidential aspirations, the tone of coverage changed decidedly. A milk producers' strike in New York City became a cause célèbre for the Hearst *American* and the *Journal,* which both hyped the resulting milk shortage by claiming that urban children were "starving to death" because of Smith's failure to resolve the price dispute. Cruel cartoons in the Hearst papers depicting emaciated slum children caused Smith's sick mother to protest, "My son did not kill the babies."

Not surprisingly, Smith was enraged by the assault, and called Hearst a "mean man, a particularly low type of man" and challenged the newspaper titan to a public debate, to which Hearst replied that he found "no satisfaction in the company of crooked politicians."

Smith retaliated by labeling the *American* "the Mud-Gutter Gazette," and three years later had the satisfaction of successfully blocking Hearst from a spot as Senate candidate on the Tammany-dominated Democratic ticket. Again, in 1923, when Hearst opposed the Tammany forces with a political slate of his own, an anonymous circular appeared entitled "Hearst, A Record Of Shame." No direct connection was made to Smith's side, but the governor broadly hinted about the tycoon's freewheeling, free-spending life-style.

At the 1924 Democratic convention, when Smith was locked in a mortal battle for delegate support with William McAdoo, Woodrow Wilson's son-in-law, Hearst hypocritically blasted the "boozing, bootlegging and bartending" ways of Tammany Hall, leaving no doubt at whom the salvo was aimed. The Democrats compromised with John Davis, and Republican Cal Coolidge crushed him in the general election.

Although Hearst would sometimes forgive personal grudges and hire newsmen who'd been critical of him, he never forgot Smith's stubborn reluctance to knuckle under. Eight years later, in 1932, he labored mightily to hand the Democratic nomination

Created as a means of funding the first transcontinental railroad, the Credit Mobilièr corporation became a profit machine for its well-connected investors, who included prominent members of Congress. The New York *Sun* called the company's successful efforts to influence Congress "the most damaging exhibition of official and private villany and corruption." The controversy had dragged on for years after its revelation, beginning in 1872, when Garfield was head of the House Appropriations Committee.

A religious, self-made man who nevertheless had displayed weaknesses for financial and sexual temptation, Garfield had been told by a close friend, "Judge" Jeremiah Black, that the Credit Mobilièr story would "turn out to be the most enormous fraud that has ever been perpetuated." Don't defend its officials, Black warned, as they had intended to "corrupt" members of Congress with gifts of highly profitable stock to get their way.

Unfortunately for the nervous Garfield, the Credit Mobilièr's chief influence-peddler, Oakes Ames, had kept careful accounts of his corporation's favors on Capitol Hill. After Garfield testified that he had shied away from accepting stock or money because of his concerns over the railroad controversy, Ames produced records that purported to show that Garfield had indeed received ten shares of Credit Mobilièr stock, and that Ames had paid a $329 profit to him by check. Ames also refuted Garfield's assertion that he had borrowed money from the lobbyist.

When Garfield subsequently ran for president in 1880, his former mentor Black was so disgusted by his friend's incomplete and contradictory version of events that he supported the Democratic candidate: more damagingly, he publicly claimed that Garfield had waffled and not told the truth in order to protect other Republicans who'd been caught up in the mess. An investigating committee believed Ames's account books and concluded that Garfield had taken the $329, but offered no censure for his testimony, which obviously was considered false.

To voters who asked "What's 329?," the anti-Republican forces answered, "That's what Garfield got from the Credit Mobilièr." Democratic dirty trickers also publicized a phony letter in which Garfield was supposed to have declared his support for cheap Asian labor.

Tortured by the years-long episode, and the butt of political cartoonists, Garfield nonetheless was elected to the White House over his Democratic opponent, General Winfield Hancock. When he was shot by an unstable office-seeker less than 200 days after taking office, Garfield grimly hung on to life for two months and became a folk hero for his courageous determination.

PECK'S BAD BOY

Bespectacled and silver-haired, the middle-aged president Woodrow Wilson looked more like the college professor he once had been than a passionate lover boy. An unexpected affair of the heart, however, almost derailed his reelection bid in 1916.

Wilson had always preferred the company of women over men, and had been happily married to his gentle wife Ellen for more than a quarter century when she died of a chronic kidney disease in August 1914 while they occupied the White House. "God has stricken me almost beyond what I can bear," the despondent president wrote to a friend.

Inconsolable for months, the chief executive was barely able to carry out his duties and became so morose that aides fretted over his fragile health. His misery was abated somewhat when he was introduced to Edith Bolling Galt, an attractive, fortyish widow, seven months after his wife's death. Almost immediately, he fell head over heels in love, and penned daily, breathless love letters that read more like the gushings of a mooning teenager than the heartfelt affections of a scholarly intellectual.

"God has indeed been good to me to bring a creature such as you into my life. Every glimpse I am permitted to get of the secret depths of you I find them deeper and purer and more beautiful than I knew or dreamed of" . . . . is just a sample of the adoration Wilson felt for the widow Galt.

The overweening infatuation revitalized Wilson's spirits; almost overnight, however, public sympathy for the grief-stricken

chief executive was transformed into suspicion over his boyish, determined courtship of Edith, who at first resisted Wilson's proposals of marriage, but finally agreed to marry her ardent admirer. Rumors circulated that Wilson had been a philanderer, even while married; his nastier critics whispered that the president and Mrs. Galt had an affair before Ellen's death, and that the discovery of the illicit liaison drove the First Lady to her deathbed.

Wilson's inner circle of aides panicked; their former college don was quickly becoming a lascivious skirt-chaser in the opinion polls, and the image could wreck his chances to be reelected in 1916. Wilson's advisers told their leader that the "Peck affair" had been resuscitated. The former Mrs. Peck, or Mary Hulbert, as she was also known, was a divorcée with whom Wilson had established an innocent friendship in 1907. Despite a complete lack of evidence that their relationship was anything more than another of the many warm friendships Wilson had with a number of women, Mrs. Peck had been hounded by reporters for months prior to the 1912 election.

Now, White House aides incorrectly told the president, she was prepared to sell her private correspondence with him to eager Republicans. The phony blackmail tale failed to dissuade Wilson from pursuing his new lady love Edith, and he won reelection in a close vote over Charles Evans Hughes. Controversy remained close companion for his second wife, however. She was the target of exaggerated rumors that she was a meddlesome "Mrs. President" who supposedly took control of the White House when illness incapacitated the chief executive for much of his second term.

CITIZEN HEARST VS. THE "CHILD KILLER

One of the ugliest, most long-standing blood feuds in the history of American politics was played out for more than a dozen years between the mercurial press baron, William Randolph Hearst and Al Smith, New York's governor and an unsuccessful candidate for president in 1928. Their mutual loathing thwarted Hearst's own political ambitions and helped deny Smith a second chance at the White House in 1932.

to House Speaker John Nance Garner, and ultimately helped to deliver the vote to Franklin D. Roosevelt, a man he didn't particularly want in the White House. An unhappy Smith, still smarting over the years-long sting of being labeled a child killer by Hearst's yellow journalists, saw his national political career come to an unfulfilling end.

SCORE ONE FOR HERSCHEL

A Democratic candidate for governor of Iowa was damaged but not defeated by unfounded criminal allegations that were more than twenty years old by the time he entered the race in 1956. Herschel Loveless realized every candidate's nightmare when his Republican opponents circulated a flyer featuring a 1934 newspaper story from the *Ottumwa* (Iowa) *Courier* that detailed allegations that he'd been arrested and jailed for embezzling $450 from the oil company where he worked.

While Loveless indeed had been accused initially, he'd also been completely cleared of the charges within hours after the real thief was apprehended. Not surprisingly, his campaign opponents failed to include the subsequent story exonerating him, related author and public relations executive Bruce Felknor. The attempted smear backfired and Loveless went on to overcome it and his rather unlikely sounding name to win the election.

MOGUL POLITICS

Muckraking writer Upton Sinclair revealed the filthy, disgusting conditions in America's meat-packing plants in his celebrated exposé, *The Jungle*. In 1934, when he ran as a Democrat for the U.S. Senate in California, however, he found where the real jungle was—in Hollywood. Reactionary movie industry executives, fearful of the liberal Sinclair's promise to levy higher taxes on their industry, organized a multimillion-dollar, all-out campaign to defeat the reformer.

Democrats had complained previously that the arch-conservative Hollywood bosses had leaned on their employees to support

Republicans in the presidential races of 1928 and 1932, but it wasn't until Sinclair's campaign directly threatened their pocketbooks that the small but powerful oligarchy of film chieftans banded together to practice what writer Ronald Brownstein termed "mogul politics."

First, the studio titans suggested they might pack up and desert California if Sinclair was elected and pressed unwanted taxes on their highly profitable business. False stories were spread that Sinclair was an advocate of free love and an opponent of organized religion. Thousands of billboards proclaimed that the writer intended to turn the state over to the Depression's legion of unemployed if elected.

MGM president Louis B. Mayer pressured movie theaters to run newsreels slandering Sinclair. One of the anti-Sinclair promotions showed a humble, hardworking woman proclaiming her support for Republican candidate Frank Merriam, while Sinclair's backer was portrayed as a tattered, immigrant hobo who said with a heavy foreign accent, "His system worked vell in Russia, so vy can't it vork here?"

Sinclair's subsequent drubbing at the polls ushered in a new era of political activism by Hollywood power brokers anxious to protect their self-interest, and willing to spend unprecedented amounts of money to do it.

ETYMOLOGY OF A SLUR

"How can you vote for a man who looks like the bridegroom on a wedding cake?" That stinging description of two-time presidential candidate Thomas Dewey is generally attributed to Alice Roosevelt Longworth, the sharp-tongued daughter of Teddy Roosevelt. However, in a letter to writer William Safire, Alice admitted she didn't coin the cruel phrase; she merely helped popularize it. More likely, the quip originated with one of the three following people: columnist and society gossip Walter Winchell, Ethel Barrymore, or a friend of Alice's identified only as "Mrs. Flandrau."

Created as a means of funding the first transcontinental rail-road, the Credit Mobilièr corporation became a profit machine for its well-connected investors, who included prominent members of Congress. The New York *Sun* called the company's successful efforts to influence Congress "the most damaging exhibition of official and private villany and corruption." The controversy had dragged on for years after its revelation, beginning in 1872, when Garfield was head of the House Appropriations Committee.

A religious, self-made man who nevertheless had displayed weaknesses for financial and sexual temptation, Garfield had been told by a close friend, "Judge" Jeremiah Black, that the Credit Mobilièr story would "turn out to be the most enormous fraud that has ever been perpetuated." Don't defend its officials, Black warned, as they had intended to "corrupt" members of Congress with gifts of highly profitable stock to get their way.

Unfortunately for the nervous Garfield, the Credit Mobilièr's chief influence-peddler, Oakes Ames, had kept careful accounts of his corporation's favors on Capitol Hill. After Garfield testified that he had shied away from accepting stock or money because of his concerns over the railroad controversy, Ames produced records that purported to show that Garfield had indeed received ten shares of Credit Mobilièr stock, and that Ames had paid a $329 profit to him by check. Ames also refuted Garfield's assertion that he had borrowed money from the lobbyist.

When Garfield subsequently ran for president in 1880, his former mentor Black was so disgusted by his friend's incomplete and contradictory version of events that he supported the Democratic candidate: more damagingly, he publicly claimed that Garfield had waffled and not told the truth in order to protect other Republicans who'd been caught up in the mess. An investigating committee believed Ames's account books and concluded that Garfield had taken the $329, but offered no censure for his testimony, which obviously was considered false.

To voters who asked "What's 329?," the anti-Republican forces answered, "That's what Garfield got from the Credit Mobilièr." Democratic dirty trickers also publicized a phony letter in which Garfield was supposed to have declared his support for cheap Asian labor.

Tortured by the years-long episode, and the butt of political cartoonists, Garfield nonetheless was elected to the White House over his Democratic opponent, General Winfield Hancock. When he was shot by an unstable office-seeker less than 200 days after taking office, Garfield grimly hung on to life for two months and became a folk hero for his courageous determination.

PECK'S BAD BOY

Bespectacled and silver-haired, the middle-aged president Woodrow Wilson looked more like the college professor he once had been than a passionate lover boy. An unexpected affair of the heart, however, almost derailed his reelection bid in 1916.

Wilson had always preferred the company of women over men, and had been happily married to his gentle wife Ellen for more than a quarter century when she died of a chronic kidney disease in August 1914 while they occupied the White House. "God has stricken me almost beyond what I can bear," the despondent president wrote to a friend.

Inconsolable for months, the chief executive was barely able to carry out his duties and became so morose that aides fretted over his fragile health. His misery was abated somewhat when he was introduced to Edith Bolling Galt, an attractive, fortyish widow, seven months after his wife's death. Almost immediately, he fell head over heels in love, and penned daily, breathless love letters that read more like the gushings of a mooning teenager than the heartfelt affections of a scholarly intellectual.

"God has indeed been good to me to bring a creature such as you into my life. Every glimpse I am permitted to get of the secret depths of you I find them deeper and purer and more beautiful than I knew or dreamed of" . . . is just a sample of the adoration Wilson felt for the widow Galt.

The overweening infatuation revitalized Wilson's spirits; almost overnight, however, public sympathy for the grief-stricken chief executive was transformed into suspicion over his boyish, determined courtship of Edith, who at first resisted Wilson's proposals of marriage, but finally agreed to marry her ardent admirer. Rumors circulated that Wilson had been a philanderer, even while married; his nastier critics whispered that the president and Mrs. Galt had an affair before Ellen's death, and that the discovery of the illicit liaison drove the First Lady to her deathbed.

Wilson's inner circle of aides panicked; their former college don was quickly becoming a lascivious skirt-chaser in the opinion polls, and the image could wreck his chances to be reelected in 1916. Wilson's advisers told their leader that the "Peck affair" had been resuscitated. The former Mrs. Peck, or Mary Hulbert, as she was also known, was a divorcée with whom Wilson had established an innocent friendship in 1907. Despite a complete lack of evidence that their relationship was anything more than another of the many warm friendships Wilson had with a number of women, Mrs. Peck had been hounded by reporters for months prior to the 1912 election.

Now, White House aides incorrectly told the president, she was prepared to sell her private correspondence with him to eager Republicans. The phony blackmail tale failed to dissuade Wilson from pursuing his new lady love Edith, and he won reelection in a close vote over Charles Evans Hughes. Controversy remained a close companion for his second wife, however. She was the target of exaggerated rumors that she was a meddlesome "Mrs. President" who supposedly took control of the White House when illness incapacitated the chief executive for much of his second term.

CITIZEN HEARST VS. THE "CHILD KILLER"

One of the ugliest, most long-standing blood feuds in the history of American politics was played out for more than a dozen years between the mercurial press baron, William Randolph Hearst, and Al Smith, New York's governor and an unsuccessful candidate for president in 1928. Their mutual loathing thwarted Hearst's own political ambitions and helped deny Smith a second chance at the White House in 1932.

When the Tammany-backed Smith took office in early 1919, Hearst's hard-charging news organization accorded the new governor a honeymoon of sorts. Within a few months, however, perhaps because Hearst felt the popular Smith represented a threat to his own presidential aspirations, the tone of coverage changed decidedly. A milk producers' strike in New York City became a cause célèbre for the Hearst *American* and the *Journal,* which both hyped the resulting milk shortage by claiming that urban children were "starving to death" because of Smith's failure to resolve the price dispute. Cruel cartoons in the Hearst papers depicting emaciated slum children caused Smith's sick mother to protest, "My son did not kill the babies."

Not surprisingly, Smith was enraged by the assault, and called Hearst a "mean man, a particularly low type of man" and challenged the newspaper titan to a public debate, to which Hearst replied that he found "no satisfaction in the company of crooked politicians."

Smith retaliated by labeling the *American* "the Mud-Gutter Gazette," and three years later had the satisfaction of successfully blocking Hearst from a spot as Senate candidate on the Tammany-dominated Democratic ticket. Again, in 1923, when Hearst opposed the Tammany forces with a political slate of his own, an anonymous circular appeared entitled "Hearst, A Record Of Shame." No direct connection was made to Smith's side, but the governor broadly hinted about the tycoon's freewheeling, free-spending life-style.

At the 1924 Democratic convention, when Smith was locked in a mortal battle for delegate support with William McAdoo, Woodrow Wilson's son-in-law, Hearst hypocritically blasted the "boozing, bootlegging and bartending" ways of Tammany Hall, leaving no doubt at whom the salvo was aimed. The Democrats compromised with John Davis, and Republican Cal Coolidge crushed him in the general election.

Although Hearst would sometimes forgive personal grudges and hire newsmen who'd been critical of him, he never forgot Smith's stubborn reluctance to knuckle under. Eight years later, in 1932, he labored mightily to hand the Democratic nomination to House Speaker John Nance Garner, and ultimately helped to deliver the vote to Franklin D. Roosevelt, a man he didn't particularly want in the White House. An unhappy Smith, still smarting over the years-long sting of being labeled a child killer by Hearst's yellow journalists, saw his national political career come to an unfulfilling end.

SCORE ONE FOR HERSCHEL

A Democratic candidate for governor of Iowa was damaged but not defeated by unfounded criminal allegations that were more than twenty years old by the time he entered the race in 1956. Herschel Loveless realized every candidate's nightmare when his Republican opponents circulated a flyer featuring a 1934 newspaper story from the *Ottumwa* (Iowa) *Courier* that detailed allegations that he'd been arrested and jailed for embezzling $450 from the oil company where he worked.

While Loveless indeed had been accused initially, he'd also been completely cleared of the charges within hours after the real thief was apprehended. Not surprisingly, his campaign opponents failed to include the subsequent story exonerating him, related author and public relations executive Bruce Felknor. The attempted smear backfired and Loveless went on to overcome it and his rather unlikely sounding name to win the election.

MOGUL POLITICS

Muckraking writer Upton Sinclair revealed the filthy, disgusting conditions in America's meat-packing plants in his celebrated exposé, *The Jungle*. In 1934, when he ran as a Democrat for the U.S. Senate in California, however, he found where the real jungle was—in Hollywood. Reactionary movie industry executives, fearful of the liberal Sinclair's promise to levy higher taxes on their industry, organized a multimillion-dollar, all-out campaign to defeat the reformer.

Democrats had complained previously that the arch-conservative Hollywood bosses had leaned on their employees to support

Republicans in the presidential races of 1928 and 1932, but it wasn't until Sinclair's campaign directly threatened their pocket-books that the small but powerful oligarchy of film chieftans banded together to practice what writer Ronald Brownstein termed "mogul politics."

First, the studio titans suggested they might pack up and desert California if Sinclair was elected and pressed unwanted taxes on their highly profitable business. False stories were spread that Sinclair was an advocate of free love and an opponent of organized religion. Thousands of billboards proclaimed that the writer intended to turn the state over to the Depression's legion of unemployed if elected.

MGM president Louis B. Mayer pressured movie theaters to run newsreels slandering Sinclair. One of the anti-Sinclair promotions showed a humble, hardworking woman proclaiming her support for Republican candidate Frank Merriam, while Sinclair's backer was portrayed as a tattered, immigrant hobo who said with a heavy foreign accent, "His system worked vell in Russia, so vy can't it vork here?"

Sinclair's subsequent drubbing at the polls ushered in a new era of political activism by Hollywood power brokers anxious to protect their self-interest, and willing to spend unprecedented amounts of money to do it.

ETYMOLOGY OF A SLUR

"How can you vote for a man who looks like the bridegroom on a wedding cake?" That stinging description of two-time presidential candidate Thomas Dewey is generally attributed to Alice Roosevelt Longworth, the sharp-tongued daughter of Teddy Roosevelt. However, in a letter to writer William Safire, Alice admitted she didn't coin the cruel phrase; she merely helped popularize it. More likely, the quip originated with one of the three following people: columnist and society gossip Walter Winchell, Ethel Barrymore, or a friend of Alice's identified only as "Mrs. Flandrau."

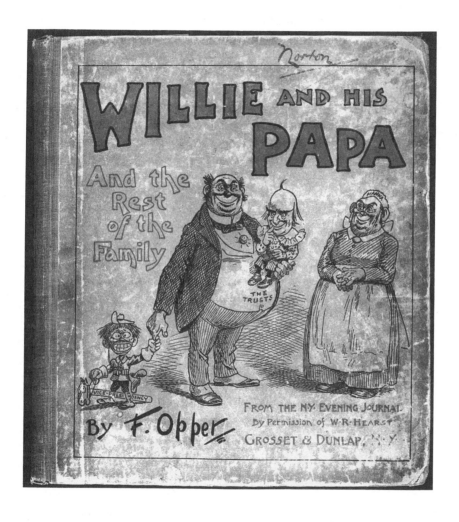

If it wasn't the fast-talking Winchell, he got off another shot at Dewey when he described the diminutive former New York governor and crusading prosecutor as the "only man able to walk under a bed without hitting his head."

FALA'S REVENGE

By 1944, Franklin D. Roosevelt had been president for almost a dozen years, and his political adversaries were growing increasingly desperate to find a means—any means—of dislodging the charismatic Democrat from the White House. The frustration of GOP nominee Thomas Dewey and his campaign team was revealed by their determination to use an unproven charge, aimed at embarrassing FDR, which boomeranged right back at the Republicans in one of the more noteworthy rebuttals in American political history.

Dewey's minions asserted that, during an inspection tour of Alaska, President Roosevelt had left his pet dog "Fala" behind in the remote Aleutian Islands, and that a U.S. warship had been sent, at taxpayer expense, to retrieve the chief executive's favorite mutt. Unfortunately for Dewey, FDR quickly deflated the possible controversy by directly appealing to millions of American dog lovers with his usual, dry wit:

> "These Republican leaders have not been content with attacks on me, or my wife, or my sons. No, not content with that, they now include my little dog Fala. Well, of course, I don't resent attacks, and my family doesn't resent attacks, but Fala *does* resent them."

Richard Nixon was "the kind of politician who would cut down a redwood tree, and then mount the stump and make a speech for conservation."
—Adlai Stevenson

LIKE FATHER, LIKE SON

Franklin D. Roosevelt, who had a genius for pitting his advisers against each other, wasn't above employing questionable tactics to punish his political adversaries. In a critical 1960 Democratic presidential primary, his son and namesake showed that he'd learned a few lessons in hardball from the old man. While he'd once been close to Minnesota senator Hubert Humphrey, one of the leading contenders for the nomination, FDR, Jr., appeared repeatedly beside rival John F. Kennedy in West Virginia, where his family name and the New Deal were political magic.

Almost pathetically, Roosevelt allowed himself to be used as a tool to attack Humphrey in a vulnerable spot—he was one of the few nationally recognized politicians without a war record. Young Kennedy, the handsome hero of PT boat 109, turned the difference in military experience to his advantage by having Roosevelt say about Humphrey, "I don't know where he was in World War II," and handing out papers provided by the Kennedy camp that falsely charged that Humphrey was a draft dodger.

Later, perhaps out of shame, Roosevelt offered Humphrey a retraction and an apology, but by then the damage had been done.

"Advance to the attack but side-step the smear. It is not a smear, if you please, when you point out the record of your opponent. Of course, it is always a smear, naturally, when it is directed at your candidate."
—MURRAY CHOTINER
NIXON ADVISER AND RENOWNED POLITICAL
GUT-FIGHTER

JOE STALIN'S PAL?

An election incident early in his career might help explain Arizona senator Barry Goldwater's career-long disdain for both or-

ganized labor and what used to be the Soviet Union. In his first
Senate race in 1952, against the popular Democratic incumbent,
Ernest W. McFarland, Goldwater came under fire from the unions
for helping to pass the state's right-to-work law. Late in the
campaign, when Goldwater's rise in the polls threatened his
better-known rival, flyers were passed out to the voters that
showed a caricature of the Soviet dictator Joseph Stalin winking
and asking: "Why Not Vote for Goldwater?"

Goldwater's opponents claimed that he and his Republican
cohorts had distributed the Stalin flyers themselves to win sympathy. But the prank backfired after Goldwater went on television
to deny the charges; he ultimately won a 7,000-vote upset victory
"on Ike's (Eisenhower's) coattails," as he put it.

THE BAKER AND JENKINS HOUSE

By the final few weeks of the 1964 presidential campaign, it was
apparent that the Republican ticket, Arizona senator Barry Goldwater and his running mate, the obscure, wisecracking New York
congressman William Miller, had little or no chance of defeating
the Democratic team of President Lyndon Johnson and Senator
Hubert Humphrey. But that didn't stop the more reactionary of
Goldwater's conservative supporters from hurling every brickbat
at their disposal in the direction of LBJ, a man they intensely
despised.

Scandalmongers hoping to sway undecided voters against
Johnson got a big break about a month before election day when
one of the president's key aides, Walter Jenkins, was arrested,
along with an older man, for "disorderly conduct (indecent gesture)" in a men's washroom at the YMCA across the corner from
Lafayette Park near the White House. A loyal aide who'd served
Johnson for twenty-five years, Jenkins, it turned out, had been previously arrested in 1959 at the same location on similar charges.

At the time of his preelection arrest, he was said to be utterly
exhausted from months of overworking. Soon afterward, he entered a hospital for observation, while Democratic power brokers

quickly tried to head off damaging publicity concerning Jenkin's aborted sexual misadventure.

Presidential advisers, including prominent Washington attorney Clark Clifford, were at first successful in convincing news editors to hold off on publishing any stories recounting the details of the humiliating episode. Rumors of Jenkins's encounter with the Washington police department's vice squad reached the Republican camp, however, and GOP national chairman Dean Burch cleverly if cruelly exposed the attempted cover-up. Without referring to Jenkins by name, Burch hyperbolically alluded to "a report sweeping Washington that the White House is desperately trying to suppress a major news story affecting the national security."

Soon Jenkins's private habits became a public issue; LBJ's foes spread false whispers that homosexuality was rampant in the Johnson administration, and that well-known Democrats had engaged in other sexual shenanigans. The influential James Reston, chief of the *New York Times* Washington Bureau, intoned that the revelation of Jenkins's 1959 arrest "seriously embarrassed" the Johnson administration, and raised national security questions concerning why the ranking White House aide had not been further investigated at the time. "Walter Jenkins has revived and dramatized all the harsh feelings about morals, and political cliques, and the Texas gang in Washington, and this clearly can do the President no good," Reston wrote in a story that sent chills down the spines of Johnson campaign supporters.

Former vice-president Richard Nixon also jumped into the fray: "The question is why Johnson kept Jenkins in spite of an earlier apprehension on a morals charge in 1959," he said.

Meanwhile, phony anti-Johnson "three dollar bills" and other counterfeit campaign currency were circulated. One bill had a picture of the White House labeled the "Baker and Jenkins House," referring to both the arrested White House aide and Bobby Baker, another Johnson assistant who was in trouble over allegations of influence-peddling, and to whom Jenkins had been linked months earlier during a congressional investigation. "Johnson is King and Jenkins is a 'Queen,' " was one of the nastier slogans that circulated.

The hubbub ultimately had no measurable impact on the election race, which ended with a resounding victory for Johnson, but its unfortunate timing served to make a preelection spectacle of the unfortunate Jenkins, who had to resign his life's work in disgrace three weeks before his president was reelected.

WITH FRIENDS LIKE THESE ...

It's bad enough when the insulting campaign doggerel is coming from the other side of the political fence. But in 1970, Republican senator Charles Goodell learned, to his chagrin, that sometimes your worst enemies are in your own camp. The New York politician was vocal in his criticism of President Nixon's conduct of the Vietnam conflict, and he was a bit of a liberal to boot. So he was targeted for defeat, not only by the Democrats, but by Nixon loyalists who wanted the Conservative party candidate—crew-cut, square-jawed James Buckley—elected instead.

The designated hatchet man was Vice-President Spiro Agnew, who seemed to relish the assignment of crisscrossing the country, blasting his president's opponents. Charging that Goodell had encouraged "the dissident elements of our society," Agnew claimed that Senator Goodell "had left his party." That was sweet talk compared to what followed, as columnist and election coverage veteran Jules Witcover noted in his book about the former vice-president.

Meeting with newspaper editors in New Orleans, Agnew tried to ridicule Goodell's Vietnam statements by claiming they were inconsistent with his views while serving in the House. "If you look at the statements Mr. Goodell made during his time in the House and compare them" to more recent pronouncements, "you will find he is truly the Christine Jorgensen of the Republican party,'' quipped Agnew, referring to the first person known to have undergone a successful sex change operation.

The cutting remark probably engendered snickers among the conservative faithful, but other Republican power brokers were not amused. ''It is a matter of the deepest regret,'' cabled Nelson Rockefeller's political adviser, George Hinman . . . ''to have our proud banner so lightly dipped in filth against another Republican whose only offense is an independent view of the issues of life and death in our time.''

Hinman wasn't the only unhappy camper. Christine Jorgensen didn't like the comparison, either. She described Agnew's performance as a ''bull in the china shop,'' and added that she didn't like being used as a ''political pawn.'' ''Mr. Agnew has a case of the 'cutes,' '' she responded indignantly.

The rebuttal didn't stop Agnew's assault, and ultimately Goodell's reelection effort failed; it bled to death from fighting a two-way campaign against both the Democrats and his ''friends'' at the White House.

A NASTY "STAR WARS" CAMPAIGN

The 1980 campaign for the congressional seat representing California's 27th District was a star-studded slugfest featuring two politicians who each had backing from major Hollywood celebrities; allegations of illegal campaign contributions; a candidate's meeting with a felon in an Alabama prison; and an angry Washington office showdown between a congressman and a U.S. senator.

The incumbent was the fiery, red-hair former fighter pilot and talk show host, Robert K. Dornan, the nephew of the late actor Jack Haley of *Wizard of Oz* fame and a darling of Tinseltown's Republican, conservative community. Opposing the flamboyant Dornan for the Democrats was movie superstar Gregory Peck's second son, Carey. The younger Peck attempted to oust the better-known Dornan from office by spending months walking around his well-manicured precinct and introducing himself to voters with the greeting, "Hi. I'm Carey Peck. I'm running for Congress. How're you doing?"

Those were probably the most civil words spoken during the campaign. Referring to Peck as a "sick, pompous little ass," Dornan hammered at his opponent about previous illegal contributions from an Alabama businessman who was serving time in federal prison for fraud. During an earlier campaign against Dornan, Peck had received $13,000 from James Dennis, a twenty-eight-year-old wheeler-dealer who'd met his famous father at a political fund-raising dinner at Birmingham's Hugo's Rooftop restaurant.

Unfortunately for Peck, Dennis had lied about collecting the contributions from individual donors and instead had given all the money himself, a violation of federal campaign laws. Dennis also had appeared on ABC-TV's "20/20" program and claimed he'd served as a bagman to channel bribes to state coal operators. Peck said he returned all the checks to Dennis when he learned they were tainted.

That was far from the end of the controversy, however. When a Federal Election Commission inquiry into the disputed contributions didn't settle the matter to his satisfaction, the outspoken Dornan went on the warpath. Taking his wife Sallie, he flew to Alabama and visited Dennis at the Talladega correctional institution in the presence of an FBI representative and other witnesses. According to the congressman's account, the young con man said he had taken back the campaign checks and then handed Peck the same amount in cash, an assertion the film star's son hotly denied.

The plot thickened when Dornan attempted to ask Dennis about his campaign contributions to Alabama senator Donald Stewart (D), whom he suspected had steered Dennis to Peck in the first place. That would be impossible, Justice Department officials informed the surprised Dornan, as there was an active federal investigation under way of Senator Stewart's finances. Shortly afterward, Dornan discovered to his shock that Sen. Stewart had been granted a private meeting with Dennis at Talladega just days after his own escorted visit. His loud, public complaints about an alleged cover-up of the Alabama money trail to California eventually led to what he described as a shouting match between the two legislators in Stewart's Capitol Hill office.

Stewart's supporters then cleverly turned the tables on the freewheeling Dornan by making available recordings of several telephone conversations during which the congressman seemingly had suggested special favors for inmate Dennis if he came clean about the dirty campaign money. Dornan was blasted by the influential *Los Angeles Times* for taped statements such as: "I made a promise to Dennis that if he helped me I'd help him and I am trying to keep my end of the promise for selfish reasons as well as humanitarian reasons." Prison officials steadfastly maintained that Dennis received no VIP treatment.

When Dennis later denied having said that he'd handed over illegal campaign cash to Peck, Dornan admitted regret over making the issue into a cause célèbre. Despite all the negative hoopla, he again narrowly defeated Peck in the general election, and the fast-talking Dennis waltzed out of jail after serving only four months.

The forty-year-old Stewart, who'd gained his seat in a special election in 1978 following the death of the legendary Sen. James Allen, was the ultimate loser. Although his campaign was cleared of possible violations of federal financing laws by the Justice Department, questions about his relationship with the slippery Dennis persisted. Reports of the FBI probe into his personal finances contributed to his loss that fall to a younger Democratic primary opponent.

THE GURU AD

The 1986 gubernatorial election in Pennsylvania may well have been decided at the last minute by what was commonly referred to as the "guru ad." The race was a squeaker, pitting lawyer and veteran Democratic office-seeker Bob Casey against the scion of the Keystone State's Republican establishment, Bill Scranton. Young Scranton was the state's lieutenant governor and the namesake of one of the best-known names in GOP political circles. His politically popular father had been governor, United Nations ambassador, and presidential candidate. In the home stretch, Scranton's private polls showed that the election was virtually up for grabs.

During the final weeks of the bruising campaign, Casey's television ads effectively, if mercilessly, portrayed his Republican opponent as a rich, inexperienced dilettante who'd been born with a silver spoon in his mouth. At this point Scranton made what might have been a fatal mistake. He went on television and announced that mudslinging didn't amount to leadership; he was through with the negative campaigning that had dominated the election up to that point.

Unfortunately for Scranton, his side had already sent out a statewide mailer to hundreds of thousands of voters that contained a nasty reference to his Democratic rival. Irate, Casey seized the chance to publicly accuse his opponent of taking the low road after promising a gentler approach. The anti-Casey mailer, while "inadvertent . . . knocked the legs out from under us," recalled John Baer, press secretary for Scranton's running mate, state senator D. Michael Fisher.

The controversy gave Casey's side an opening to administer the coup de grace on the last weekend of the campaign. They launched the so-called guru ad. Opening up with psychedelic sitar music, the televised advertisement showed a younger Bill Scranton with long hair, and intoned that he'd been given family newspapers to manage, a venture in which he'd supposedly failed miserably. How then, according to the implication, could he help to manage the state's budget? Next, Scranton was portrayed as a disciple of transcendental meditation and a follower of the Marharishi Yogi, not exactly a popular figure with older, more conservative voters.

The spot, targeted for airing in the state's more rural areas, made Scranton look like he wanted to "impose kookiness on the people of Pennsylvania," and was like a "kick in the groin," remembered Baer, who noted that the eleventh-hour blitz made it impossible to reply, as stations refused to accept additional ads

ALL SET FOR THE CAMPAIGN!

before the vote. "Tactically, it was a masterpiece" of negative campaigning, conceded Baer, now a statehouse reporter for the *Philadelphia Daily News*.

Despite complaints that the clever if transparent ad was a cheap shot, Scranton went on to lose an exceedingly close election.

HERE'S WHAT WE'LL DO TO YOUR OPPONENT

"Meet Edwin Eisendrath III, the Democrat's [sic] Dan Quayle," blared the red, bold-faced headline on a campaign brochure ridiculing a young Chicago city councilman who dared to challenge a fellow Democrat, senior Congressman Sidney Yates, for his seat. While the pamphlet portrayed Eisendrath as a spoiled rich kid "who doesn't seem to take his job seriously," the most interesting feature of the handout was that it was never circulated or mailed out.

In a disclaimer in small print on the back of the brochure, Bates & Associates, a political consulting firm, noted that it was "a design composite only." The firm's client, they explained, "abandoned the basic attack tenets of modern campaigning in favor of remaining a gentleman; in other words, our client decided not to mail out this piece."

"We respect his opinion," stated the consultants, "because nobody should ever mail out anything that makes them uncomfortable. But, we decided to have this piece printed to show those who, for some reason, think we're too nice to do hard-hitting negative or 'comparative' mail. And, because we really like it."

We got the message.

WATCH WHAT YOU SAY IN ILLINOIS

With his trademark bow tie and glasses, Democrat Paul Simon looks more like a precocious schoolboy than a fire-breathing politician. But both he and his handsome, patrician Republican opponent, Senator Charles Percy, dropped all pretense of politeness when they squared off and traded charges of false advertising during their 1984 campaign in Illinois.

When Percy aired a commercial claiming that Simon would raise taxes by $200 billion, the generally low-key Simon became enraged and rushed to a television studio to tape his own spot, in which he branded the Percy commercial as a lie.

"I'd rather lose by telling the truth than win through distortion." Later, Simon called Percy a liar to his face for running what he called "sleazy" advertisements, which he claimed were a gross misrepresentation of his plan to increase the tax burden on the wealthy and thereby reduce the federal deficit.

Smoking Simon wasn't the only one to lose his cool during the rather tempestuous campaign. Simon supporters ran a radio commercial on a black-oriented station featuring a black woman who said "we need a Senator who will stick with us, not a Senator who will take our vote and stick it to us." The usually stiff-necked Percy hit the roof and labeled the ad racist and misleading.

"I can't wait to get out of this chickenshit outfit."
—Senator James Abourezk of South Dakota, near
the close of the 1978 Senate session.

POP QUIZ

What group states in its Code of Professional Ethics that "I shall not indulge in any activity which would corrupt or degrade the practice of political campaigning," or "I will refrain from false and misleading attacks on an opponent or on a member of his family and shall do everything in my power to prevent others from using such tactics?"

(Answer: *The American Association of Political Consultants*)

However, one consultant active with the association's ethics procedures admitted in a 1991 interview that the high-sounding code "has no support process," and that complaints usually were confined to "contractual obligations" and "being paid" for consulting work rather than policing dirty tricks and negative campaign practices.

A political science professor close to the AAPC also conceded that efforts to create and enforce a practical, uniform ethics program for those who help candidates get elected "haven't moved too far," but that the group's members know they have a growing image problem with the voters and are planning to address ethics issues at future meetings.

ATWATER'S "ALLIES"

The late Republican political tricks-meister Lee Atwater didn't limit his clever and occasionally outrageous antics to Democrats. In fact, he saved a lot of his best stuff for Republican candidates who weren't conservative enough to suit him, or who stood in the way of a paying client's ascension to higher office.

Prior to the 1988 Republican presidential primary, Atwater was just as tough on his boss George Bush's rivals for the GOP nomination as he later was on Massachusetts governor Michael Dukakis. For example, at the Conservative Political Action Conference, then-Representative Jack Kemp (R-NY), a presidential possibility, was lampooned as a "two-faced sellout politician" by anonymous critics who mysteriously billed themselves as the Conservative Truth Squad.

After looking into the anti-Kemp crusade, conservative commentator Fred Barnes concluded that the congressman's supporters were wrong in believing that aides to Senator Robert Dole, another Republican presidential hopeful, had been responsible for distributing the widely circulated mailing. Barnes talked to Craig Shirley, a former consultant for the Bush campaign, who charged that the energetic Atwater was the real villain behind the attempted trashing of fellow Republican Kemp. "I want it [the mailing] to happen," Shirley quoted Atwater as saying prior to the conservatives' get-together.

Shirley further asserted that he quit the Bush campaign over the backstabbing attack on Kemp, and that his earlier public pronouncement that he was "merging" his consulting firm with that of David Keene, a senior Dole adviser, was just a cover story to divert questions about his resignation and to avoid embarrassing the Bush forces.

Barnes noted that the faceless accusations against Kemp violated the spirit if not the letter of the campaign laws, which state that anyone making a campaign expenditure who "advocates the election or defeat of a clearly identified candidate" should "identify himself or herself," so that the audience knows who paid for the viewpoints.

That wasn't all that Shirley disclosed about Atwater's underhanded tactics against others in his own party organization. In 1986, Shirley asserted, he was asked by Atwater to leak disparaging information to the _New York Post_ concerning Ed Rollins, formerly Atwater's boss at the White House political office and later Kemp's campaign chairman. Finally, Shirley charged that he was asked to get one of his conservative friends not tied to the Bush campaign to sign a campaign complaint against Kemp at the Federal Election Commission. To back this charge, he provided to Barnes a six-page draft of the complaint composed by a lawyer working for the Bush campaign.

The glib Atwater denied Shirley's detailed allegations; and characteristically, tried to turn the tables on his accuser by suggesting that Shirley himself had probably been behind the assault on Kemp. "Shirley's the guy with the list," Atwater claimed, referring to Shirley's partner Keene's job as head of the American Conservative Union, which would have given him access to the names and addresses of hundreds of right-wing activists.

"If all of this sounds slightly absurd," summarized Barnes, "it is."

SKINNY-DIPPING

Unlike some states, where the politics of the personal can get brutal, Minnesota's voters had always prided themselves on campaigns that were generally as pristine as the state's ten thousand lakes. At least that was generally the case until the 1990 gubernatorial race, an ugly affair that featured outlandish allegations and countercharges on the front pages; ultimately, the wild campaign significantly and unexpectedly altered the balance of power in the state capital.

About a month before the election, character became an important issue. Republican candidate Jon Grunseth, who was trying to unseat Democrat Rudy Perpich, was accused in affidavits by two women of encouraging them to remove their bathing suits and swim in the nude with him at a backyard pool party nine years before. At the time, the women were only thirteen and fourteen years old. Outraged, Grunseth denied the allegations, and called his opponent a "supreme liar" for denying that he'd had a hand in making the charges public. Grunseth was also accused of having an extramarital affair.

Although he resisted leaving the GOP ticket for weeks, party leaders finally decided he had to go if they were to have any chance to win, even though there were only nine days left in the race. He was replaced by state auditor Arne Carlson, who managed to get elected, despite being in the campaign barely more than a week. Minnesotans didn't "have enough time to get sick of him," *Time* magazine concluded in reporting his improbable victory.

That wasn't the end of the Skinny-dipping Scandal. Grunseth felt he was unfairly forced out by biased media coverage. His former campaign manager and spokesman paid to publish several thousand copies of a book, *There Is No November*, attacking the personal life and ethics of the *Minnesota Star-Tribune* reporter who broke the skinny-dipping tale. The reporter, according to one of the authors, engaged in "vicious character assassination" and "unethical tactics." Grunseth's version of events is that one of the women making the charges against him was an admitted cocaine user, and that his supposed extramarital affair occurred between his first and second marriages.

THE CAMPAIGN FROM HELL

A seemingly desperate attempt by an Arizona Democratic gubernatorial candidate to link his Republican opponent to the savings
and loan scandal backfired in February 1991 and possibly cost
him the election. Terry Goddard, a former mayor of Phoenix,
was supposed to easily win a November 1990 general election for
the governor's seat over his politically inexperienced foe, Fife
Symington. But in a major surprise, Symington finished 4,500
votes ahead of the heavily favored Goddard and forced a runoff
election, as required by state law when no candidate gets more
than fifty percent of the vote.

Round Two set the stage for what one Arizona paper called
"slime-filled attacks." The turning point of the campaign slugfest came just weeks before the runoff election, when Democratic
senator Howard Metzenbaum (OH) entered the fray uninvited
by announcing an unusually timed congressional hearing to ex-
plore Symington's links to failed savings and loan institutions in
Arizona.

Republican legislators hit the ceiling upon learning of Metzenbaum's intrusion into the closely fought governor's contest. Senate minority leader Robert Dole (R-KS) was livid, calling the
hearing a "vicious sneak attack, a blind-side hit without fair
notice or fair play." Dole also accused Metzenbaum of helping
Goddard to make a negative campaign commercial about Symington's alleged links to S&L failures.

Symington's advisers convinced him that he had to counter-
attack quickly to avoid being fatally smeared by the Democratic
assault. His handlers conceived a tough riposte to Goddard by
airing a televised compaign commercial called "Jailyard." The
thirty-second commercial blasted Goddard for accepting a
$60,000 salary from a Phoenix law firm without actually working
for it. Since the payment might have violated the state's campaign finance laws, Symington's ad portrayed a blue-shirted Goddard, seemingly in prison garb, behind bars.

J. Brian Smith, Symington's political consultant, wrote that he
knew the controversial ad would be effective when his nine-year-

old son looked up from his toys and said that the man on television "broke the law." Indeed, the advertisement attracted statewide attention: the "campaign from hell," as one national newspaper called it, grew uglier still.

Goddard's standing in the polls plummeted after the ad ran for only forty-eight hours. But even a steady drumbeat of negative ads suggesting that Symington might be indicted for his S&L links failed to resuscitate Goddard's failing appeal, and Symington ultimately won the election.

Goddard's "attack strategy," according to a political writer for the *Phoenix Gazette*, "was simply out of sync with the Boy Scout persona he had carefully nurtured in three successive campaigns against patsy foes."

Senator Metzenbaum didn't escape unscathed, either. In retaliation for what was perceived to be his unwanted meddling, Senate Republicans ordered their investigative staffs to launch a months-long probe of Democratic ties to the chief executive of a failed savings and loan, and their final report proved embarrassing to Metzenbaum and several of his colleagues later that year.

FAMILY FEUD

Nepotism is a time-honored tradition in American politics; public-office holders have been putting family members on the payroll since colonial days. In Baltimore, however, whether hiring relatives to join the taxpayer gravy train is a sin or not depends upon your perspective.

In a 1991 political ad paid for by Citizens for Good Government, incumbent city council member Nicholas J. D'Adamo was blasted for employing his father as an administrative aide and for keeping a district office in his family's hardware store. "Mr. D'Adamo would rather hear the cash register ring than his phone," stated the advertisement, which was presented as an "open letter to the voters of the First District."

The criticism was "definitely dirty politics," complained an irate D'Adamo. "When you attack family, that's about as low as you can go. And I don't think they're in a position to throw stones.''

The offended councilman may have had a point. The treasurer of Citizens for Good Government, as it turned out, was one Louis Cavaliere, who worked for D'Adamo's opponents on the so-called Proven Team, which included another councilman, John Schaefer, whose daughter received a city salary while working for him.

''Yes, my daughter works for me,'' Schaefer conceded, ''but she earns her money. She goes to community meetings for me. Nick's father just sits in the store and answers the telephone.''

Election time was near, for the ''mud was starting to fly,'' as the *Baltimore Sun* noted.

''[He's] what a lot of Democrats have been looking for—somebody who not only matches fire with fire, but isn't afraid to use blow torches. You can criticize him on grounds of civility and gentility. But he wins.''
—University of Virginia political scientist Larry Sabato, on Democratic consultant James Carville, who helped mastermind Harris Wofford's 1991 upset victory in the Pennsylvania special election for the U.S. Senate.

CHIP OFF THE OLD BLOCK

The elder George Allen was a legendary professional and college football coach whose most well known team was the Washington Redskins' ''Over The Hill Gang.'' A tireless workaholic who was a bit on the paranoid side when it came to the motives of his gridiron opponents, Allen was famous for his willingness to do virtually anything that would give his side an edge in an important game.

Apparently his son George learned how to translate his father's penchant for sports hardball into the political arena. A lawyer and political conservative, young Allen ran as a Republican for the congressional seat in Virginia's 7th District, near Charlottesville, in 1991. His Democratic opponent, Kay Slaughter, was a cousin of the incumbent, who left Congress for health reasons.

Their contest was nothing out of the ordinary, until late in the campaign, when the coach's son aired an unusual political advertisement. It showed Slaughter's photograph displayed next to a crowd of antiwar demonstrators holding a banner that read VICTORY TO IRAQ. Allen reminded his constituents that he enthusiastically supported American military incursion into Kuwait, while Slaughter had opposed it.

The unspoken implication of the ad, however, seemed to be that Charlottesville city councilwoman Slaughter was allied with unpatriotic, "radical liberals"; she called the insinuation a "despicable lie." Since the National Republican Congressional Committee produced the ad, Slaughter charged that her constituents were "being used as guinea pigs by the Republican Party's specialists in negative campaigning."

Outraged, Slaughter marched up to the Iwo Jima war memorial in Virginia. with the offending ad and Tennessee senator Albert Gore in tow. At an impromptu press conference, she indignantly denounced Allen for attempting to unfairly label her as an anti-American war protester: the apple-cheeked, tousle-haired Gore, who had supported the White House decision to invade the Middle East, backed her up with a soothing, on-the-spot testimonial.

That wasn't the end of the media show, though. Soon after, Allen made an appearance with his own entourage, which included telegenic, white-haired Virginia senator John Warner. Grouchily, Warner snapped at television photographers that he wouldn't pose in front of the memorial, claiming that Slaughter had used it for political purposes (which, of course, was also his reason for being there). Then he rebutted Slaughter's criticism by saying he didn't think there was anything wrong with the controversial ad, except the "technical" problem that

Slaughter didn't actually *attend* the specific rally featured in Allen's ad.

Whether or not the embarrassing sideshow had any effect on the result, Allen won handily. The day *after* the election, he apologized for linking his opponent to the controversial Iraqi protest banner.

THE POLITICAL DANCING JACK:
A Holiday Gift for Sucking Whigs!!.
Sold at No. 104 Nassau, and No. 18 Division Streets. New-York.

DIRTY TRICKS

YOU CAN'T MAKE ASSES OUT OF US

The image of the donkey, now widely accepted as a symbol of the Democratic party, was originally used to cruelly ridicule its candidates. The use of a mule to lampoon Democratic office holders apparently began in the 1830s; the original target was President Andrew Jackson.

Anti-Jackson critics liked to remind voters that the "Old Hero" from Tennessee, while a genuine war hero, was a bit on the uneducated side. When Harvard University bestowed the unlettered Jackson with an honorary doctor of law degree, his opponents distributed metal campaign tokens for the 1834 congressional elections that poked fun at the award. One side contained the printed phrase, "The Constitution As I Understand It," encircling a donkey's profile with the imprint "LL.D." An 1837 cartoon, "The Modern Balaam And His Ass," depicted Jackson prodding his stubborn donkey, with his successor, Martin Van Buren, bringing up the rear.

In 1848, the Democrats' unsuccessful candidate for president, Lewis Cass, was caricatured as a mule, with the caption "Brother, Beware, C-ass." During the Civil War, the Republicans utilized the donkey to symbolize the Democratic "Copperheads," who had sympathy with the Confederacy, according to the research of Tim Coughlin of the Democratic Political Items Collectors.

Actually, it wasn't until the 1896 elections that the donkey began to become a positive emblem for the Democrats, when it was used on the campaign buttons promoting their young, golden-throated orator, William Jennings Bryan, for president.

A BRUISING ELECTION DAY

Many campaigns have been described as "slugfests," but Election Day 1856 was literally a knock-down, dragged-out fight in many sections of the country. Ballot boxes were destroyed, and voters battled each other at the polls. The physical confrontations weren't limited to a few manly fistfights—bricks, knives, and guns were also brought into the head-smashing frays.

A *New York Times* reporter wrote that one unfortunate supporter of presidential candidate Millard Fillmore was approached at the polls by toughs representing the Democratic ticket and asked to show his voting ticket, which he refused to do. "They then forcibly took his ticket from him, tore it up and tendered him a [James] Buchanan and [Mayor] Wood ticket, saying he must vote it or none. He again declined, when he was immediately felled by a blow, was beaten and dragged out."

In another polling location, a voter had his nose shot off. Dozens of thugs from the anti-immigrant Know-Nothing party engaged in ferocious hand-to-hand combat with opponents from other parties. The indiscriminate violence made it impossible for the sheriff to find enough men willing to risk their lives to control the mobs, according to the account of author Denis Tilden Lynch.

STANTON'S SPIES

Union General George B. McClellan ran for president on the Democratic ticket against his own commander in chief, Abraham Lincoln, in 1864. The Democrats believed that the dashing, popular young military commander, still in his thirties, would put them back in the White House. Both parties wanted to end the four horrific years of Civil War bloodshed: but Lincoln insisted that one of the unshakable preconditions to a lasting peace was the abolition of slavery. In accepting the party's nomination, McClellan agreed to the Democrats' platform, which called for peace negotiations as soon as one or more of the Confederate states agreed to rejoin the Union.

To put it mildly, the Democrats' peace plan didn't thrill one of Lincoln's more suspicious Cabinet members, Secretary of War Edwin Stanton. McClellan became convinced that Stanton and his minions spied on him throughout the campaign. "My steps are dogged & every person reported who comes to see me," he wrote to a friend. Perhaps overcautiously, he used codes when writing anything confidential, and employed personal messengers wherever possible.

His paranoia climaxed over a tip that Stanton and the administration had information about a secret conspiracy "by friends of McClellan" to assassinate Lincoln. He ultimately dismissed the reports of the alleged plot as unfounded, but still felt that Stanton's iron hand was somehow behind the whisper campaign intended to defame him as a possible traitor to the Union.

McClellan managed to poll 45 percent of the popular vote, but won the electoral votes of only three states. Ironically, the soldiers' votes he was counting on receiving went overwhelmingly to Lincoln, a total repudiation of the Democrats' Chicago peace platform, which was utterly rejected by supposedly war-weary Union forces.

DIRTYING THE NEW DEAL

As Franklin D. Roosevelt ran for his second term in 1936, his foes at the Republican National Committee were busily digging up allegations of waste, fraud, and abuse at New Deal projects across the country. The GOP's sleuths had contacts in practically every state, including newsmen who got paid salaries and expenses to uncover problems in FDR's massive social assistance programs. Republican agents masterminding the anti-Roosevelt operation in Washington also distributed their findings to sympathetic radio broadcasters eager to undercut the Works Progress Administration and other Democratic-backed relief agencies.

Their undercover gumshoe work wasn't of much help to their party's hapless candidate, Kansas governor Alf Landon, who was crushed by Roosevelt in the presidential election that fall.

THE FIRST NIXON-INSPIRED BREAK-IN?

The medical problems of John F. Kennedy were severe enough that some observers speculated about how long the young politician would be able to serve if he was elected president in 1960. During the campaign season, burglars broke into the offices of JFK's New York physicians, apparently looking for his private files. Fortunately, the records were wisely stored under another name for additional security.

While there was no evidence to link Nixon aides to the attempted theft, Republican William Casey, later Ronald Reagan's campaign manager and Central Intelligence Agency director, investigated Kennedy's medical condition for Nixon during the campaign. Casey had a well-known penchant for bold—even illegal—covert action, which came back to haunt Reagan during the Iran-Contra scandal. And, the Nixon team developed a taste for break-ins, including the office of the psychiatrist of Pentagon Papers leaker Daniel Ellsberg in 1971. In retrospect, it's made many wonder if the unsuccessful theft was possibly the first black bag job of several to follow, including the Watergate building.

DIRTY POLITICS DOES NOT PAY

Unlike baseball, politics isn't totally obsessed with statistics. But once in a while, it's valuable to take stock of what pitches your opponents are using most often. In 1966, the Washington-based Fair Campaign Practices Committee did just that. Committee staffers studied 51 of 505 congressional and governors' races across the nation to attempt to learn what kinds of negative election attacks were employed, and the relative success of each.

The investigators found evidence that of a "routine type" of dirty politics in more than half of the cases they examined: 35 percent of the complaints filed in the sample studies claimed "misinterpretation," or "distortion" of at least one candidate's election message. Another 17 percent of the candidates charged their opponent with some form of "personal vilification" during the campaign.

A frequent cause of unhappiness among candidates for public office was alleged violation of campaign laws, or the breaking of postage or mailing regulations; that complaint was cited in 16 percent of the committee's case studies. Almost one in seven, or 14 percent of the office-seeking hopefuls, moaned that they were accused of "guilt by association" by their opponents—the smears ranged from being linked to the Communist party to charges of sympathy with the far-right John Birch Society.

Allegations of racial prejudice (12 percent) and religious bigotry (6 percent) were less common. But disturbingly, the committee's analysis noted that while by the mid-sixties, overt race-baiting seemed to be dying out, new "code words" implying racism were becoming more popular with candidates willing to take the low road: "busing," "violence in the streets," and "forced housing" had become the new "buzz words" of racial politics by 1966. John F. Kennedy's election in 1960 had curbed much of the anti-Catholic bias that severely damaged the 1928 presidential campaign of New York governor Al Smith, among others.

Oddly enough, the committee's conclusion was that "dirty politics does not pay." The fair campaign analysis showed that 68 percent of those who employed questionable campaign tactics lost.

BACKDOOR DIPLOMACY

A last-minute attempt by Richard Nixon's camp to influence or delay the Vietnam peace talks during the final weeks of the 1968 presidential campaign might have been the most underhanded and potentially catastrophic campaign-related trick of the decade. The nasty political fallout from the unofficial diplomatic skulduggery left Democrats and Republicans arguing for more than twenty years about what really happened and who was to blame.

President Lyndon Johnson, who previously had removed himself as a possible candidate for reelection, announced a U.S. bombing halt in Vietnam in late October, just before the vote in an extremely close contest between Hubert Humphrey and Nixon. Republican loyalists angrily termed LBJ's decision an "election-

weekend stunt'' designed to influence the hard-fought campaign in Humphrey's favor. Johnson's advisers claimed that the North Vietnamese had dropped their crucial opposition to South Vietnam's participation in the peace talks, and that the concession deserved a positive response. In a conference call in mid-October, the president notified Humphrey, Nixon, and third party candidate George Wallace of his intention to renew negotiations for a cease-fire.

What the Johnson White House didn't know until later, however, was that a monkey-wrench had been thrown into the delicate proceedings by Anna Chennault, the Chinese-born widow of a general who had commanded the famous Flying Tigers in World War II. The lovely, well-connected widow Chennault was co-chairman of the Women for Nixon-Agnew National Advisory Committee. After a private meeting with Nixon and her close friend Bui Diem, South Vietnam's ambassador to the U.S., Chennault secretly advised Diem that his country would get a better peace deal if Nixon won the election. She suggested that the South Vietnamese government stall or cripple the plan by refusing to cooperate with Washington.

Although it wasn't publicly known until well after the event, U.S. intelligence was wiretapping the South Vietnamese embassy and learned of the unwelcome, Republican-inspired meddling. The discovery put Johnson in a "cold fury," said White House aide Jack Valenti. Another presidential confidant, Max Kappelman, stated that the president believed that "this was all a Nixon conspiracy." Just before the election, Johnson privately confronted Nixon with the evidence, but he denied being involved in Chennault's illicit backdoor diplomacy.

Not wanting to admit they'd been wiretapping their allies, both Johnson and Humphrey decided not to go public with allegations that a well-known Nixon supporter had been caught trying to undermine U.S. foreign policy. Longtime presidential election chronicler Theodore White later wrote that "Humphrey might have won the presidency if he'd gone public" with the charges. Instead, he lost one of the closest elections of modern times.

THE BOSS OF BOSSES

At the height of his considerable power, Chicago mayor Richard Daley was arguably the most influential local politician in America: Democratic candidates for state and even national office entered Daley's office reverently and humbly, as though it was the Vatican and its occupant the pope. Dispensing patronage became an art form during Daley's lengthy tenure as the political world's boss of bosses.

Before the city's infamous vote-grabbing "Machine" assured his empire, however, Daley had been just another ward heeler who'd managed to push Mayor Martin Kennelly to an early and unwanted retirement in 1955. Seizing the Democratic nomination for himself, Daley turned his Democratic Machine's minions loose to execute a campaign of dirty tricks against their formidable Republican opponent, Alderman Robert Merriam.

Never reluctant to hit below the belt, Daley's lieutenants attacked Merriam's personal life. The alderman had been divorced from his college sweetheart; copies of the divorce papers were circulated in conservative Catholic neighborhoods, according to an account by Chicago columnist and longtime Daley-watcher Mike Royko. Not content with that underhanded stab, the Machine's lackeys sent out letters claiming no one knew how many children Merriam might have abandoned without support. Daley's hit men also went after Merriam's second wife, who was French-born, by passing false preelection whispers that she was part black.

Letters from the non-existent "American Negro Civic Association," related Royko, were sent into heavily white residential areas, urging a vote for Merriam because he supposedly promised that blacks would be provided homes and building opportunities all over the city in an era when Chicago was still effectively segregated. A liberal, Merriam was also the victim of another phony letter from the "Taft-Eisenhower League" accusing him of associations with left-wingers.

Standing apart from the handiwork of his party's henchmen, Daley beat his first mayoral opponent by 120,000 votes and started an unprecedented age of one-man rule in the City of Big Shoulders.

MAULING MUSKIE

The Offensive Security Program was the formal title given to a highly successful political dirty tricks operation, established by President Richard Nixon's minions to confuse and sabotage various Democratic presidential candidates in the early 1970s.

Senator Edmund Muskie of Maine, a statesmanlike and articulate legislator, was the man most feared by the Nixon forces as an obstacle to their leader's reelection in 1972. The unlucky Muskie, therefore, was the unwitting target of the Nixon campaign group's most imaginative pranks.

Getting an early start against their foe, the Nixon operatives recruited a taxicab driver in 1971 and planted him as a spy inside Muskie's presidential campaign headquarters. Elmer Wyatt portrayed himself as an eager volunteer for Muskie while earning $500 a month from the other side to sneak out memos and campaign schedules and deliver them to an ex-FBI agent named John "Fat Jack" Buckley. In turn, Buckley obligingly handed over the smuggled goods to Nixon campaign aides Jeb Stuart Magruder and Bart Porter.

The following year, on the campaign trail, Muskie had flight trouble on a West Coast trip because the pilot followed false instructions and brought the astonished candidate to an unscheduled stop in Salem, Oregon. A phony flyer printed on Muskie's stationery and widely circulated accused fellow Democratic candidates Henry Jackson and Hubert Humphrey of sexual improprieties, hurting him as well as his distinguished Democratic colleagues.

The besieged senator was also the victim of a forged letter using the offensive term "Canuck," which made it appear as though he condoned racial slurs. When the rumors began to include Muskie's wife Jane, it was enough to make a man break down and cry, which he finally did before a stunned and uneasy campaign audience. His brief lapse of control, while understandable, was captured on videotape and its repeated broadcast effectively finished him as a presidential contender.

SEDAN CHAIR I AND II

Not all of the Nixon team's carefully planned array of dirty tricks and political sabotage were successful; in fact, at least one of the so-called "black advance" operations was intended to be limited to pranks and low-level disruption of Democratic campaigns, according to former Nixon aide Jeb Magruder.

"Sedan Chair" (named after a Marine military exercise) involved relatively harmless stunts such as arranging for pro-Nixon signs to greet Democratic candidates like Senator Edmund Muskie when they arrived at the airport. Magruder contends that phase one of Sedan Chair required the expenditure of less than $4,000, and ended in several months when the young operative hired to carry out its rather mundane objectives, Californian Roger Greaves, quit because he disliked the work.

Not giving up easily, though, the Nixon hit men opened up a second chapter of Sedan Chair and hired a private detective from Kentucky, whose main mission was to spy on the Pennsylvania primary campaign of Hubert Humphrey. The Minnesota politician's effort in the state was a "disaster," with few volunteers and no organization, wrote Magruder, so disrupting it was totally unnecessary. Nixon campaign manager John Mitchell and Magruder had a "good laugh" at Humphrey's expense after reading their undercover spy's report. Sedan Chair II, claimed Magruder, was intended as "comic relief in the serious business of reelecting a President."

The once boyish-looking Magruder served seven months for perjury and obstruction of justice as a result of the Watergate investigation, and is now a Presbyterian minister.

THE PRINCE OF PRANKSTERS

For many years, the man Republicans loved to hate was Californian Dick Tuck. The Democrats' unofficial merry prankster tortured many a GOP candidate with his imaginative practical jokes, although the most famous and frequent target of his colorful campaign stunts was longtime nemesis Richard Nixon.

"A legend in his spare time," is how veteran Tuck-watcher Morris Siegel described the mischievous political jokester. His reputation for the unexpected was well deserved, and by the Watergate era, various word-of-mouth snippets of Tuck lore had reached almost mythic proportions in the smoke-filled barrooms and crowded campaign offices where election war stories are swapped.

One of Tuck's most memorable ploys to embarrass the opposition occurred in 1964, when he planted a young female spy aboard Senator Barry Goldwater's campaign train. The attractive interloper ("a cute pixie," Goldwater later conceded) slipped on to the "Goldwater Special" at Washington's Union Station, posing as a reporter.

That night, while most passengers were asleep, the Democratic Mata Hari, whose name was Moira O'Connor, distributed copies of a pamphlet called The Whistle Stop, which included, among other tidbits, the solemn declaration that for the duration of the trip, the conservative Goldwater would remain on Washington time—_George_ Washington time, that is. Journalists traveling with the Goldwater entourage were delighted with the mysterious diversion from routine campaign speeches; but Vic Gold, one of the candidate's press aides, was not so amused. Catching Tuck's plant red-handed with additional copies of The Whistle Stop, he told O'Connor, "This is your last stop, dear," and unceremoniously put her off the train in Parkersburg, West Virginia. "I hope she had bus fare," Goldwater later dead-panned.

Other Tuck pranks may not have happened, but true or not, they have been repeated so often they have become part of American political legend. Ever the eternal adolescent, Tuck seemed to have a childlike fascination with trains. The highlight of his high jinks against archenemy Nixon in the 1960 presidential campaign came while the candidate was in Santa Barbara, California, addressing a rally from the rear of his own whistle-stop special. Off to one side stood Tuck, dressed in a conductor's uniform, waving a red lantern. "Okay, pull her out," he shouted, while Nixon's surprised audience watched in stunned silence.

Media critic Jeff Greenfield recalled another 1960 Tuck-inspired ego-deflater; after the famous "5 o'clock shadow" debate with JFK he had a woman with a big NIXON campaign button run up to the suddenly perplexed and unnerved vice-president and say, "Don't worry, you'll do better next time."

On yet another occasion, when Nixon visited Los Angeles's Chinatown, Tuck was reported holding a banner proclaiming WELCOME, NIXON in English, while in Chinese script was the message, "What about the Hughes' loan?", referring to a controversial deal between billionaire financier Howard Hughes and Nixon's black sheep brother Donald. During Nixon's unsuccessful 1962 gubernatorial race against Democrat Pat Brown in California, his press aides were convinced that Tuck was spying on Nixon and reporting back to the Kennedy White House on his every move.

A decade later, Tuck was still antagonizing Nixon. At the 1972 Republican National Convention in Miami, when a group of seemingly very pregnant women were circling outside the convention hall, shouting and wearing buttons embossed with the candidate's best-known campaign slogan, NIXON'S THE ONE, Tuck got the blame.

Tuck's years of taunting got under Nixon's skin. When the Republicans' own dirty trickster, Donald Segretti, got into legal trouble for hounding Democratic politicians with a variety of illegal acts, Nixon was irritated at what he considered an unfair double standard. Tuck's pranks, he complained in his *Memoirs,* were merely considered "good clean, fun, but where we were doing it, it is grim and vicious espionage and sabotage of the worst type." Ironically, claimed former Nixon aide John Ehrlichman, Segretti was originally recruited by the White House to be "our Dick Tuck."

THE KILLER INSTINCT

Perhaps Richard Nixon's most hard-nosed political operative was Charles Colson. Once immortalized for supposedly claiming that he would run over his grandmother to get Nixon reelected (Colson staunchly denied the quote, but later embraced it as a sign of his toughness), he believed in the maxim, "Do unto others before they do unto you." His White House colleague Herb Klein wrote that Colson had "the killer instinct."

Colson's enmity toward Democrats who opposed Nixon was especially sharp in the case of Maryland senator Joseph Tydings. In 1970, Colson obtained information from a private attorney linking Tydings with allegations of influence peddling. He leaked the information to *Life* magazine, then in trouble and desperately in need of a circulation boost, and a highly critical story was published late into the campaign season. After the election, according to Klein, the story was disproved, but Tydings already had lost.

That wasn't enough for Colson, who organized a fund-raising committee of Republicans, a few of whom didn't know their names were being used, whose advertising theme was: "What kind of man is Joe Tydings?"

Convicted of obstruction of justice charges in connection with Watergate, Colson underwent a moral transformation and organized a prison ministry. Still, his own memoirs were subtitled *"What Really Happened to the White House Hatchet Man?"*

A TAXING PROBLEM

In a meeting held in the White House during the 1972 campaign, Richard Nixon with aide H. R. Haldeman and White House counsel John Dean debated how to get the secret tax records of Democrats targeted for political retribution. "We have to do it artfully so that we don't create an issue by abusing the IRS [Internal Revenue Service] politically," Nixon warned his subordinates. "And, there are ways to do it. Goddamn it, sneak in in the middle of the night . . ."

While Haldeman fretted that the Nixon team shouldn't "take the risk of getting us blown out of the water before the election," he demonstrated no reluctance to pursue the illegal obtaining of confidential tax information. "Let the Democrats down there squeal and say Nixon's pulling out the tax files of all the Democrats . . . let them scream about repression and all that stuff."

At one point, Dean offers what he hopes will be a helpful suggestion: "The other thing is you could always increase your [tax] compliance program . . . just happens that a lot of Democrats get caught."

"Well," concluded Nixon, warming to the thought, "they're going to get it . . . we've got to do it, even if we've got to kick [IRS commissioner Johnnie] Walter's ass out first and get a man in there."

WHAT THE NIXON CREW *DIDN'T* DO

Richard Nixon's White House–directed dirty trickers did pull off an impressive string of election-related break-ins, buggings, harassment, and just plain pranks on their political enemies. But it's noteworthy that not *all* of their sometimes harebrained plots were translated into actual deeds. For example, Gordon Liddy, the tight-lipped paramilitary operator who was fond of holding his hand over a candle flame to show his disdain for pain, had far more grandiose ideas about how to stop his president's opponents than he was ever able to launch into operation. For once, Liddy's wacko proposals were shot down before they could become part of the Nixon reelection campaign of 1972.

On January 27, 1972, at a White House meeting to discuss the administration's blueprint for campaign hardball, a solemn-faced Liddy stood before several large, multicolored easels to outline his goofball game plan to save the Republic. First, Liddy told his listeners, who included Attorney General John Mitchell, White House counsel John Dean, and campaign deputy Jeb Stuart Magruder, "Operation Diamond" would address their worries about noisy, disruptive convention demonstrations against their boss. Liddy proposed drugging any radicals who showed up (he specifically mentioned "Yippie" leaders Jerry Rubin and Abbie Hoffman), and using CIA operatives to abduct the longhairs and hold them in Mexico until the convention was over.

To upgrade spying techniques on the Democrats at their Miami convention, Liddy proposed docking a sixty-foot yacht, wired for sound, directly in front of the luxurious Fontainebleau Hotel. Any prominent Democrats they could lure aboard, including those "vulnerable to weakness of the flesh," would be tempted by a bevy of prostitutes who would be living on the floating brothel. When Dean objected that the strategy amounted to a rather foolhardy attempt at extortion, Liddy irritatedly replied, "[T]hese are the finest call girls in the country . . . I can tell you from first-hand experience . . ."

Another chart, detailing "Operation Sapphire," outlined plans for shutting down the air-conditioning ducts in the convention center, so that the unsuspecting Democrats would be "sitting there dripping wet in one hundred and twenty-degree heat on national television!"

This was all too much even from the pipe-puffing Mitchell, known to possess one of the nastiest curveballs in politics. "Well, Gordon, that's all very intriguing, but not quite what I had in mind," Mitchell concluded, literally sending Liddy back to the old drawing board.

The eager intelligence operative came back a few weeks later with a toned-down version of his James Bond schemes, which culminated in the Watergate break-in and cover-up.

DIVORCE, CONGRESSIONAL STYLE

A number of congressional spouses have tried to carry on their mate's work by running for a seat vacated by illness or death. Not too many former congressional wives ran *against* their ex-husbands, though, until Louise Synder came along. She and her husband, Kentucky Republican representative Gene Synder, went

through a messy and public divorce battle in 1973. Their split, while not a political boost in Bible-belt Kentucky, didn't keep the well-entrenched Gene from running for reelection in 1974.

When the congressman married his former office manager, however, Louise took off the kid gloves according to an account in the book *The Power Lovers*. She announced she would run for Congress against her ex-husband. Her motive, she confessed, was not public service. She wanted Gene to cancel a suit seeking custody of their fourteen-year-old son. "I don't care about politics," Louise admitted candidly. "I'm doing this to protect my son."

Gene wasn't exactly chivalrous himself. "I've done a little research on that new husband of hers," he countered. "If she runs against me I'll get the court to release the divorce file and they'll both have to leave town." Louise wailed that the custody fight was "rigged" because of her former spouse's political clout. He told a reporter that his would-be challenger was using publicity to get at him, and he threatened to release what he regarded as an incriminating photo of his ex-wife and her new partner.

Louise decided not to pursue the election after the bruising, fifteen-round custody battle, and Gene was reelected.

DEPENDS ON YOUR PERSPECTIVE

Nixon speech writer, conservative commentator, and presidential candidate Patrick J. Buchanan has never been one to mince words when it comes to facing down critics of his former boss, but he believed some campaign-related sins were worse than others. Here's what he told the Senate Watergate Committee in September 1973:

"My own view is that there are four gradations. There are things that are utterly outrageous and I would put that in with the kind of demonstrations against [Democratic presidential candidate Hubert] Humphrey in 1968 which denied him an opportunity to speak for almost a month. Then, there is 'dirty tricks.' Then, there is political 'hardball.' Then there is pranks.'"

Buchanan's mentor Nixon contended that there was a double

standard in operation by which his supporters' attacks were always judged as loathsome dirty tricks, while the hardball tactics employed by his adversaries were laughed off as harmless by his critics in the press.

MO THE RADICAL?

Retired Arizona congressman Morris "Mo" Udall was one of the most beloved members of Congress. His self-effacing, folksy wit and easy-going manner, together with a gift for legislative accomplishment, made him a favorite of reporters and his colleagues on both sides of the aisle. Mo's undeniable personal popularity, however, didn't stop his political opponents from painting him at election time as an out-of-step liberal who cared more about what was going on under the Capitol Dome than back in his sun-drenched congressional district.

In 1978, two years after unsuccessfully running for the Democratic presidential nomination, Udall was ripe for defeat, in the view of his detractors. Arizona Republicans decided to play hardball with the veteran legislator. Udall's opponent, Tom Richey, commissioned a television advertisement that stated that the Democrat "doesn't . . . think like us anymore."

As proof that he was out of touch, Udall was seen in the ad declaring that "I'm for socialism because I think the owners of public lands ought to be paid something." Admitting to being a socialist in Arizona is about as popular as confessing to child molestation. The televised snippet, as respected political scientist Larry Sabato noted, was a deliberate misrepresentation of Udall's comments. Accused of a "socialist" approach to the sale of public lands by a critic at the videotaped gathering, Udall had actually said, "If paying the American public for their land is socialism, then I'm for socialism because I think the owners of public land ought to be paid something."

Udall's opponent refused to withdraw the ad even after the distortion was pointed out. He won reelection anyway, but his 54 percent vote was the lowest Udall had recorded in his seventeen years in Congress.

TABLE FOR TWO, PLEASE

When Republican representative John Anderson of Illinois jumped into the 1980 presidential sweepstakes as an independent candidate, it was the Democratic incumbent president, Jimmy Carter, who was nervous about losing votes to the bespectacled, white-haired Republican congressman. Carter's backers did all they could to sabotage Anderson's third party movement, for they correctly figured that Anderson would siphon off many more votes from their man than from Republican Ronald Reagan.

In New Jersey, reported muckraking columnist Jack Anderson, Democratic party officials made certain that Anderson's name appeared on the ballot behind the Socialist and Communist party candidates. White House officials also quietly urged banks not to loan money to the grassroots Anderson campaign. The behind-the-scenes effort to undermine Anderson didn't keep Carter in the White House, however; his own candidacy was hurt far more by a sagging economy, the Iran hostages fiasco, and in-fighting within his own divided party, than by the quixotic efforts of the mild-mannered Midwestern legislator.

THE OCTOBER SURPRISE

The seizure and months-long captivity of more than fifty hostages from the American embassy in Iran produced perhaps the nastiest examples of campaign subterfuge seen during the 1980 presidential campaign. With Jimmy Carter and Ronald Reagan running nip-and-tuck in the polls during the final weeks of the campaign, both Republican and Democratic strategists became convinced to the point of paranoia that the hostage issue would decide the election, one way or another.

Reagan's lieutenants, led by their crusty, wily political campaign manager, William Casey, were convinced that the Carter White House would try a last-minute, preelection "October Surprise" to get the hostages released, and salvage President Carter's flagging image with the American public. His political standing had been badly damaged by an aborted desert rescue attempt costing eight U.S. servicemen's lives.

On the other side, Carter's nervous handlers suspected that Casey and his minions would stop at nothing to keep the hostages from being released until the votes were cast and their man had assumed residency in the White House. The mutual finger-pointing had the campaign thick with rumors of a last-minute military action or covert deal concerning the hostages, whose fate was a daily soap opera being played out on national television.

In fact, a new nightly ABC news program, Ted Koppel's "Nightline," was launched as a vehicle for keeping the public informed about the latest tidbits concerning the plight of the unfortunate captives. Investigative stories, including a series of columns by syndicated writers Jack Anderson and Dale Van Atta, detailed supposed plans by the Carter White House for another military rescue attempt, reports strongly disputed by the president's aides. Whatever the reality, the hostages were not released until a White House Rose Garden ceremony held just after Ronald Reagan took office in January 1981.

More than a decade after the controversy, former Carter aide Gary Sick, an ex-member of the National Security Council, publicly asserted that Reagan campaign executives had actively plotted to keep the hostages in involuntary bondage until after the election. More than a dozen witnesses, according to Sick, had provided statements placing the peripatetic Casey at meetings in European hotels during which the fate of the hostages was discussed with representatives of the Iranian government of the Ayatollah Khomeini. It was an open secret that, despite their hatred of the U.S., the mullah's messengers desperately wanted arms and supplies for their holy war against Iraq's Saddam Hussein. Democrats charged that Republican sources promised to supply such weaponry through Israel if the radical clerics cooperated and held off releasing the hostages until *after* the election.

The charges and countercharges flew back and forth throughout 1991, with one former Reagan campaign aide calling the unproven allegations an "obscenity." While the credibility of some of the witnesses, several of whom were jailed felons and arms merchants, was dubious, Congress organized a special task force to prove the inconclusive testimony about Reagan's supposed version of the October Surprise.

PILFERED PAPERS

During the summer of 1983, a congressional subcommittee chaired by Democrat Rep. Donald Albosta, a Michigan farmer, investigated allegations that Ronald Reagan's presidential campaign unfairly benefited from the use of confidential briefing materials stolen from the files of President Jimmy Carter's White House.

The charges had been floating around as a result of offhand comments made near the end of the presidential election race almost three years before. During the final week of the 1980 campaign, Michigan congressman David Stockman revealed to a luncheon audience in Elkhart, Indiana, that he'd used a "pilfered copy" of Carter's debate briefing book to prepare Reagan for the upcoming, historic presidential debate between the two candidates.

Stockman, later to become Reagan's budget director, told his audience that Reagan's advisers used the purloined papers to rebut the five "white lies," which he said the Democrats would make the centerpiece of their debate strategy against the Republican nominee. The boyish-looking Stockman related that the "white lies" included untrue charges that Reagan was an "extremist" and a "warmonger." When Carter's line of attack followed Stockman's confident prediction, the Democrats cried foul and demanded to know how their closely held plans had leaked to the enemy camp.

Nothing was done about the so-called "Debategate" affair, however, until Albosta's aides became intrigued with news and book accounts outlining the alleged campaign rip-off, which remained unsolved. In fact, it had been barely mentioned since Reagan assumed office. The staffers convinced their boss to launch a year-long inquiry into the allegations, despite cries of sour grapes from Republicans understandably reluctant to have the controversy rekindled prior to the 1984 elections.

After months of digging, hundreds of interviews, and an exhaustive FBI check for fingerprints, the subcommittee produced a 1,500-page, two-volume, five-pound report that confirmed that Reagan's campaign had gone after and gotten a ton of papers, memos, reports, and files from inside the Carter administration, much of which was considered highly confidential.

Among the jewels of the Reagan campaign's haul, according to the congressional investigators, were sheaves of White House briefing materials used to prepare President Carter for the debate. Two Reagan aides were even found to have copies of a 250-page "big book" on Carter foreign policy in their personal files. This study, outlining the president's policy objectives and the likely response from the opposition, had been prepared by high-ranking Democratic White House staff aides working in the strictest secrecy during nights and weekends.

The Reagan activists also had acquired the "Mondale papers," a loosely organized collection of briefing materials on foreign policy and national security. Copies of the Mondale papers were found in the personal files of senior Reagan adviser Frank Hodsoll and were used to prepare the vice-president for a possible vice-presidential debate with Reagan running mate George Bush, which was never held.

"The Carter debate briefing papers were used by persons connected with the Reagan-Bush campaign to enhance Governor Reagan's performance in the debates. The persons using the papers were aware that they were using Carter debate briefing papers," stated the congressional report.

However, the subcommittee's tireless probe didn't solve the key mystery—Who smuggled the Debategate papers to the Reagan campaign in the first place? A list of possible suspects was compiled, and for a few days headlines suggested that the theft was a sex-for-secrets swap: Someone in the Reagan camp had been sleeping with a Carter aide who had access to the eyes-only materials. That juicy tidbit was discredited almost as quickly as it surfaced, though, and no political traitors were positively identified. Nevertheless, investigators conceded that several key witnesses hadn't been "entirely candid" about who they talked to and when.

The most likely culprit in the heist, concluded the congressional bloodhounds, was former CIA director William Casey, then Reagan's campaign manager. The irascible Casey claimed that he wouldn't have touched the briefing papers "with a ten-foot pole" after several Reagan colleagues pointed the finger at him as the source of the papers. But the investigation revealed that Casey had actively sought Carter materials for use by Reagan insiders, and that it was probable, in the words of the report, that the " 'big book' and the 'Mondale papers'—entered the Reagan-Bush campaign through its director, Casey."

Republican members of the Albosta subcommittee loudly denounced the inquiry as a waste of time and taxpayer money, and a three-page Justice Department report dismissed the inconsistencies among witnesses as explainable by "differences in recollection or interpretation."

WINDY CITY RUMORS

Even by the rough-and-tumble standards of Chicago politics, the 1983 mayoral campaign between Democratic congressman Harold Washington and Republican state legislator Bernie Epton was a bruiser. Race was a dominant, if largely unspoken factor, and handbills emphasizing demeaning racial stereotypes were widely circulated in an effort to discredit the black candidate, Washington. At the same time, his conviction for failing to file federal income taxes and a suspension of his law license didn't do much for the outspoken Washington's image.

Despite the ugly race-baiting atmosphere surrounding the campaign, however, the most underhanded tricks were unleashed just before the election. Two weeks before the vote, an anonymous leaflet circulated, which charged that the influential _Chicago Tribune_ had suppressed an explosive story that Washington once had been arrested for molesting a young boy. The candidate's

arrest record supposedly had been expunged from police files. But the leaflet claimed that the arresting officer and the family of the child could confirm the incident.

Fortunately for Washington, an enterprising television reporter traced the leaflets to Epton campaign volunteers. When the *Tribune* decided to print a story about the phony leaflet, stressing that there was no evidence to support the slur against Washington, the last-minute stunt backfired and gained sympathy for the Democrat, who won in a close vote.

WHAT, LICENSE US?

Political consultants like to pontificate about running clean campaigns, but apparently it's another matter when they're faced with regulation of their often less-than-professional behavior. Californian Dan Stanford made that unhappy discovery in 1985.

A conservative, buttoned-down Republican, Stanford was serving as chairman of the state's Fair Political Practices Commission (FPPC). The young, University of Southern California–educated lawyer was appalled by a series of questionable campaign tactics employed during the 1984 elections in California.

One consulting firm, for example, mailed out information on a client's tax-cutting initiative with the stern warning on the front, "Property Tax 1984 Statement. Do Not Destroy." Another company circulated information about its clients that was labeled "Democratic Voter Guides," giving the misleading impression that it had the official endorsement of the Democratic party. A San Francisco columnist wrote that "recent campaigns seem to have been run by the consulting firm of 'Hoodwink, Snooker, & Lie.' "

In a modest effort to combat the rising tide of complaints pouring into his office, Stanford proposed that political consultants disclose their financial interests; their business relationships with their clients; and finally, establish guidelines for ethical conduct. His ultimate goal, said Stanford, was for the consultants to "police themselves."

It wasn't long before all hell broke loose. "Tyranny," charged one consultant, denouncing the proposal. "McCarthyism," snorted another critic, who happened to be a former FPPC chairman representing the political consulting industry. "They took out after me," Stanford recalled. They "likened me to Hitler." Stanford debated the merits of the proposals "up and down the state," but the controversial package was killed in the legislature after an unmerciful pounding by outraged editorialists thumping their chests about free speech.

"It [regulation] will happen eventually," predicted an older but wiser Stanford, now in private practice in San Diego.

NEXT TIME I'LL GO TO THE LIBRARY

Long Island Democratic candidate Michael Sullivan tested the boundaries of campaign ethics when he paid female investigators in 1986 to meet his opponent, Republican congressman Raymond McGrath, in a restaurant and secretly tape-record the conversation. Apparently the challenger had a hunch that his foe, who was separated from his wife at the time, had developed a fondness for the nightlife in Washington. The stealthy Sullivan wound up with fourteen hours of tape for nearly $18,000, nearly a third of his election war chest.

The taped tidbits didn't do Sullivan much good on the campaign trail, and many of his own party colleagues blasted him for the covert spying. However, as political analyst Frank Lutz noted, the really gutsy move came when Sullivan listed the payments on his Federal Election Commission form as "research." McGrath was reelected and is still in Congress.

THE NASHUA FOUR

George Bush might have been elected president eight years earlier if it hadn't been for a clever piece of campaign skulduggery during the 1980 Republican primaries. He was the victim of an ambush engineered by John Sears, the take-no-prisoners manager of Ronald Reagan's ultimately successful crusade to capture the GOP nomination.

At the time of the crucial New Hampshire primary, Reagan was forging ahead of a suddenly vulnerable Bush and other Republican hopefuls in the opinion polls. Hoping to benefit from the political drama of a one-on-one confrontation between the two front-runners, _Nashua Telegraph_ newspaper executives agreed to sponsor a debate at a local high school.

That's when the wily Sears decided to throw a fly into the ointment. Since the Reagan campaign had agreed to pick up the costs of the debate after Bush balked at sharing them, Sears decided to invite the other Republican candidates, including Senators Howard Baker and Bob Dole, and Congressmen Phil Crane and John Anderson (who later would carry his message in the general election as an independent).

"The governor [Reagan] wants to open up the debate" and include his fellow politicians, Sears told a stunned Jim Baker, Bush's right-hand man. To his shock, Baker quickly realized that Sears's matter-of-fact statement was more than a request: Reagan had brought his Republican opponents, soon dubbed the "Nashua Four," to the high school gym site with him. The crowd, smelling a delicious, all-out intra-party brawl, sided with Reagan and demanded that the unexpected guests be seated as participants in the debate festivities.

Stubbornly, Bush would have none of it. Looking straight ahead without expression, he angrily rejected entreaties from intermediaries urging him to yield and speak to his rivals. "I've worked too hard for this and they're not going to take it away from me," he snapped peevishly. A bit steamed up himself, Reagan already had decided to boycott the proceedings and walk out with the others if Bush refused to allow them to take part.

The debate moderator, a _Telegraph_ editor named Breen, then sealed the unlucky Bush's fate by attempting to have Reagan's microphone turned off. "I'm paying for this microphone, Mr. Green," announced Reagan to the boisterous, cheering crowd, who ignored the fact that their unexpected hero had botched his adversary's name.

Although the other candidates soon left and he got his way, the petulant Bush took a double pounding for his whining behavior and his lackluster performance against Reagan in the subsequent, anticlimactic debate. "He choked up," confessed one of his advisers.

The resulting rush of positive publicity for Reagan handed him a victory and destroyed the early momentum in favor of Bush, which undermined his once-promising candidacy. His stiff, un-yielding performance also hurt Bush in Reagan's eyes and almost cost him the vice-presidency. Only after former president Gerald Ford adamantly refused Reagan's repeated entreaties to run with him at the GOP convention did the nominee offer the number two spot to the eager Bush for the good of the ticket.

Ironically, though the planned conflagration in New Hamp-shire may have catapulted him to the Oval Office, Reagan later fired its architect, Sears, and his two top aides, Charlie Black and Jim Lake, supposedly for excluding other longtime Reagan con-fidants from campaign decision making.

A POLITICAL CONSULTANT'S LAMENT

The political world is chock-full of clever consultants who reap six-figure annual incomes in return for their sage campaign ad-vice. During election years, the prominent in the profession often become more influential than the clients clamoring for their ex-pert services. "We've become more and more important and more and more powerful and it's wrong," Democratic consultant Raymond Strouther warned a March 1991 gathering of the Amer-ican Association of Political Consultants.

Not all members of this hard-charging, media-savvy informal brotherhood end up dispensing electoral bromides at pricey Washington watering holes, however. Take John F. King, for example. The fortyish Vietnam veteran rose to the top of the Republican consulting heap in West Virginia by employing what he admitted were slash-and-burn, take-no-prisoners campaign tactics.

He relished sticking it to ranking Democrats in his home state. During one election, King related to the *Washington Post,* he collected more than 19,000 copies of an opponent's direct mail fund-raising solicitation, and mailed back the envelopes with blank pieces of paper. The reason? His rival had to pay thirty-nine cents for each one returned.

On another occasion, he spread rumors that a client's election foe was gay, an especially devastating charge in the Bible-thumping Mountain State. Later, he took delight in hearing that the man's children had gotten into fights at school over the false campaign whispers about their father. "I wanted to be Henry Thoreau as a kid," he told a reporter. "I ended up being George Patton with a little Marquis de Sade thrown in for character."

But the cocky King ran into trouble when he tried to transplant his blunt, rough-and-tumble style to Washington in 1988. Within a year, he'd lost his failing consulting business, been evicted from his apartment, and moved into a Virginia shelter for the homeless in order to survive. From his spartan room at the shelter, King confessed that he'd gone overboard in the dirty tricks department. "I was involved in politics," he reflected. "I was in a position to change things. And I just used things."

POLK & TEXAS.

BRIBERY, BLACKMAIL, AND OUTRIGHT THEFT

BELLY UP TO THE BAR

As a candidate in his early twenties, George Washington lost two elections before he was voted into the Virginia's House of Burgesses in 1758. In his first two attempts at public office, the young commander in chief of his state's armed forces made the mistake of conducting a campaign against saloons where his soldiers got too drunk to carry out their duties. By his third attempt at public office, however, he seemed to have learned a somewhat greater tolerance for the voters' love of alcohol.

Although the practice was illegal, Washington the office-seeker began providing what were known as liquid "ticklers" to prospective supporters. He didn't just buy a few rounds at the local watering hole, either—he treated the freeholders of Frederick County to 160 gallons of various liquors! Apparently, enough of them recovered from their hangovers to remember their benefactor; Washington beat out three opponents, and was reelected in 1761. In later years, the military leader-turned-politician added suppers and entertainments to his election year pitches.

YOU CAN CHOOSE YOUR OWN VALET, BEN

"When I came to power, I found that the party managers had taken it all to themselves," President Benjamin Harrison remarked at an intimate talk during which Theodore Roosevelt was present. After his election in 1888, complained Harrison, "I could not name my own Cabinet. They had sold out every place to pay the election expenses."

THE BLACK CAVALRY

A wild free-for-all over which group of grasping financiers would take control of the Erie railroad proved to be a bonanza for open handed New York legislators in 1867.

Even among the small army of robber barons of the post–Civil War era, Jim Fisk and Jay Gould stood out. They were an odd couple: Fisk was dressed in outlandish garb and openly flaunted his mistress, while the dour, calculating Gould was old beyond his thirty years and a cold fish besides. When rival tycoon Commodore Cornelius Vanderbilt decided he wanted control of Erie at any cost and began buying up its stock at a feverish pace, Fisk and Gould schemed to let the grasping industrialist have all he wanted. They set up a printing press to turn out a surplus of "watered down" paper stock, as Nathan Miller described in *The Founding Finaglers*.

The flinty commodore wasn't a man to be trifled with, though, and soon Gould and Fisk realized that they'd have to legalize the phony shares if they hoped to see their fabulous profit. Vanderbilt had effective political control in New York and had obtained a judge's order for the pair's arrest if they crossed into the state from their stronghold in New Jersey.

Always scheming for the upper hand, Gould realized that some well-placed bribes in the New York legislature would solve his problem, so with a half million dollars in cash from what he called "the India Rubber Account," he set up shop in Albany's finest hotel, the Delevan House. The most corrupt members of the state assembly were known as the "Black Horse Cavalry"; Gould and his rival "Boss" Tweed, who was greasing the wheels for Vanderbilt, tried to outbid each other for the paid favor of key lawmakers.

It was a holiday for elected graft takers. Many took money from both sides. According to Miller's detailed account, one particularly greedy bribe recipient was said to have taken $75,000 of Vanderbilt's money and then subsequently sold himself a second time to Gould for $100,000. Boss Tweed kept as many as six bars going in a suite above Gould, while he doled out hundreds of thousands of the commodore's greenbacks. When Vanderbilt's agents arrived with a fresh supply of dough for Tweed and his henchmen, Gould gave the bagman $70,000 to "do a vanishing act with the money."

After he lavished an astonishing total of around a million dollars, Gould had his victory and the watered-down stock was legalized. But in order to get Vanderbilt's process servers off his back, Gould agreed to buy back some of the artificially inflated stock that he and his partners had dumped on their unsuspecting opponent. Everyone, except perhaps the Erie's helpless stockholders, went home happy.

PUBLIC OFFICE FOR SALE: APPLY HERE

During the 1870s, patronage was king and the sale of public office wasn't the exception; it was the rule. State and local ward heelers used the "spoils system" to dole out jobs, favors, and payoffs to party loyalists. After the Civil War, the Republican party retained a stranglehold on power with its absolute control over elective and appointive sinecures. Candidates desiring office were expected to ante up a "contribution" to the party's coffers. Judgeships typically were priced at around $15,000, a seat in Congress at $4,000 (one judge apparently being worth almost four congressmen), and a place in the state legislature at a more modest $1,500, according to historian Matthew Josephson's account.

Not surprisingly, as a result of the merchandising of public office, corruption became rampant. The pervasive graft probably was worst at the nation's customs houses, which degenerated into a "scandalous system of robbery," in the phrase of reformer Carl Schurz. Although stealing flourished in customs offices around the nation, the thievery reached its zenith in New York, where the imposing, blond-maned U.S. senator Roscoe Conkling presided over a tightly organized army of patronage worker bees. When his loyal henchman Thomas Murphy resigned under fire as

Customs House chief, Conkling replaced him with the dandified Chester Arthur, a party hack and clotheshorse whose claim to fame was owning a hundred pairs of trousers.

The amiable Arthur made certain that the more than 1,000 patronage employees under his direction performed their share of campaign work and made suitable contributions to the Republican party out of their salaries. Arthur's underlings also ensured large corporate "contributions" to the Republican cause with a system of spies who, after catching importers trying to evade duties by short-weighting, would blackmail them for payoffs or additional fees instead of charging them with fraud.

President Rutherford Hayes took on the formidable Conkling in a bruising battle over control of the spoils system that lasted eighteen months. He finally managed to have Arthur and another Conkling lackey suspended from their posts and replaced by Hayes appointees.

It was far from the end of the well-dressed Arthur's political career, however; he became James Garfield's vice-president and succeeded him in the White House after President Garfield died from a fatal shot fired by a disgruntled office-seeker.

A FULL DINNER PAIL

Ohio Republican William McKinley, the originator of the famous "front porch" campaign, didn't steal the 1896 presidential election from the "Boy Orator of the Platte," Democrat William Jennings Bryan. He didn't have to—buying it was easier. President Grover Cleveland's infatuation with a gold monetary standard had become so unpopular in the recession-wracked 1890s that his own party dumped him in favor of the charismatic, thirty-six-year-old Bryan. The Nebraskan's stirring "cross of gold" speech had the Democrats jumping in the aisles of the party's packed convention hall as though it were a religious revival.

Logging an incredible eighteen thousand miles in three months, while delivering hundreds of campaign speeches and swabbing himself with gin to keep away body odor, the "Great Commoner" put on one of the most dynamic one-man shows in American electoral history. To his credit, McKinley knew he couldn't keep up with the younger, more articulate Bryan on the hustings. "I might just as well put up a trapeze on my front lawn and compete with a professional athlete as go out speaking against Bryan . . . I can't outdo him, and I'm not going to try."

There wasn't any need for the dignified governor to leave the friendly confines of his front porch. Droopy-faced Senator Mark Hanna of New York, the supreme kingmaker and defender of big-business interests, set off the clarion call of alarm on Wall Street against the crusading Bryan and raised an unprecedented war chest for his candidate. Hanna had once rescued the honest but financially careless McKinley from disaster by getting Wall Street magnates to pay off a $124,000 loan the politician had co-signed for a friend. Now he helped conjure up at least three and a half million dollars for McKinley; Standard Oil's $500,000 contribution alone was more than the total of what the Democrats could scrape together. Much of the fund-raising bonanza was spent on expensive campaign literature and mass mailings; Hanna "advertised McKinley as if he were a patent medicine," Teddy Roosevelt later remarked.

No expense was spared. Since McKinley wouldn't go out on the campaign stump, admiring audiences were brought to his home in Canton, Ohio. Train tickets home were purchased for college students who could be counted on to vote for the Republican candidate. In a technique that would be successfully repeated in later presidential elections, workers were warned by employers that their jobs would disappear if the supposedly radical Bryan was sent to the White House. "Men, vote as you please," one company official told his workers, "but if Bryan is elected tomorrow the whistle will not blow on Wednesday morning," an ominous threat in the middle of a badly sagging national economy. McKinley's promise of a "full dinner pail" sounded better to a lot of unemployed workers than another tiresome campaign discourse on the gold and silver monetary standards.

That's not to say that corruption wasn't alleged. In a book published after the campaign, Illinois governor John Altgeld charged that Bryan had been "counted out" in several states, and cited examples of instances where more ballots were recorded than voters to mark them.

McKinley's 600,000-vote victory produced the political strategy and big-business backing by which the GOP dominated presidential elections for the next sixteen years. Bryan came back for more as his party's nominee in 1900 and again in 1908, but never quite matched his stirring performance in 1896.

LUCK OF THE IRISH

If anyone ever tells you Boston isn't a tough town politically, just remind them of a few choice tidbits from the storied career of Beantown's Irish mayor, James Michael Curley. As an ambitious young man who saw an unlimited opportunity in the rough-and-tumble world of turn-of-the-century politics, Curley got himself into hot water for taking a federal exam for some less literate voters in his ward.

The would-be politician caught up on his reading and boldly ran for the city's board of aldermen while spending two months in the cooler for fraud against the federal government. He won easily after explaining to sympathetic voters that he was merely trying to help a poor workingman get a decent job to support his wife and four children. His slogan was "I did it for a friend." But when an obstinate Republican president of the board refused to seat a jailbird, Curley ran up to the second-floor office and asked the spoilsport, whose name was Whelton, if he really intended to bar him from a seat on the board. When Whelton said yes, according to writer Alfred Steinberg, Curley pointed to the window and threatened, "If you do, you will go through that window." Curley got his seat and stayed on the board for five years.

When he later ran for reelection to Congress, his favorite preelection tactic was sending boys into his district in the middle of the night to pound on doors and tell the sleepy occupants that they represented Curley's opponent and wanted their vote. Needless to say, the nocturnal raids did little to boost the chances of the anti-Curley forces.

Bored with the House and the administration of Woodrow

Wilson, Curley decided to return to the hurly-burly of Boston politics and run for mayor. The only problem was that popular John Frances "Honey Fitz" Fitzgerald (John F. Kennedy's grandfather) occupied the office and gave no indication of wanting to abandon it. Curley threw his hat in the ring despite various efforts to dissuade him by local Democratic and the Catholic church officials, who thought the impatient politician should wait his turn for higher office.

Curley knew how to get Honey Fitz to withdraw and leave the field to him. He put an ad in the newspapers that stated that he was "preparing three addresses which, if necessary, I shall deliver in the fall . . . One of these addresses is entitled: 'Graft, Ancient and Modern'; another, 'Great Lovers: From Cleopatra to Toodles'; and last, but not least interesting, 'Libertines, From Henry VIII to the Present Day.' " Honey Fitz got the message; Curley intended to talk publicly about his girlfriend "Toodles" Ryan. He reluctantly dropped out, and Curley defeated the less imaginative president of the city council.

TAMMANY'S TRICKS

The political bosses of New York's infamous Tammany Hall held a stranglehold over the city's Democratic voters for a long period in the early 1900s. Part of the Tammany machine's muscle was founded upon its complete control of thousands of patronage jobs. Those who didn't vote as they were told could quickly find themselves unemployed.

But Tammany's henchmen didn't simply count on the fear of its largely immigrant population to stay in power. Lots of imaginative tricks were devised to ensure that Tammany opponents had no real chance of upsetting its hand-picked candidates. There was, for example, the "sniff" test. A chemical with a strong, long-lasting odor was put on Democratic ballots and Tammany flunkies were assigned to sniff the exiting voters' hands. Woe be to the defector who flunked the informal vote-and-smell technique; those who didn't have the telltale stink were sure to lose their jobs or suffer other reprisals.

Then there were what writer Michael Dorman called the "repeater" voters. These were men who initially came to the polls with a beard or mustache, then returned to vote again after a local barber had shaved them or cut their hair to otherwise alter their appearance enough to fool inattentive or bribed poll watchers.

Lastly, Tammany's errand boys drew Republican voters away with the so-called "dummy polls." Impatient voters lined up and, waiting in heavily Republican districts, were politely led to fake polling places that resembled the real thing in every respect except one: their votes weren't legally recorded. The "lost," unrecorded votes helped Tammany candidates win or retain office.

Such ingenious methods weren't completely a relic of a bygone era, though. In a Republican primary election in the 1970s, one Manhattan man was arrested after he voted no less than sixty-eight times!

"The politician who steals is worse than a thief. He is a fool. With the grand opportunities all around for the man with a political pull, there's no excuse for stealin' a cent."
—TAMMANY HALL'S GEORGE WASHINGTON PLUNKITT

THE FAT FRIERS

The 1892 presidential election was about what big business wanted—and was willing to pay to get it. Downtrodden workers, increasingly disgruntled over their increasingly desperate conditions, launched a series of violent strikes throughout the country. Discontent was so rife that an assassination attempt was made on steel magnate Henry Frick. The capitalist entrepreneurs were nervous about whether the next president would maintain tariffs high enough and inflation low enough to get them profitably through what looked like a deepening recession.

The question wasn't which party would side with the rich industrialists—it was whether the Republicans or Democrats were more eager to cater to the wishes of the ruling elite. Members of both parties fell all over each other trying to curry favor with the big-business barons. Republican president Benjamin Harrison had endeared himself to the wealthy property-holders by sending federal troops to crush strikes at mines and factories across the nation.

Grover Cleveland, seeking a return to the White House after four years with the "out" party, the Democrats, realized he'd have to sidle up to the money men if he wanted to see *President* in front of his name again. Somewhat cynically, he took the advice of his campaign handler, William Whitney, to speak sympathetically of the workingmen's plight. Meanwhile, Whitney held informal meetings with industrial fund-raisers, promising political protection in exchange for generous campaign contributions. (His Republican counterparts, who pledged to bolster the already formidable tariff barriers in business's favor in return for corporate considerations, were dubbed the "fat friers.")

The Democrats quietly agreed to take care of the Sugar Trust in a deal that brought a whopping donation to the party's bulging coffers. Whitney and his cohorts also held similar sessions with banking and railroad lobbyists, extracting hundreds of thousands of dollars in contributions for unwritten promises to shield tycoons from unwanted legislative regulations and taxes.

In fairness, Cleveland may not have known the full extent of his mentor's political money-grubbing. "I have not been consulted at all—or scarcely at all—about the conduct of the campaign," he claimed on one occasion. "I don't seem to be running things much," he said another time.

Nevertheless, Cleveland's all-too-willing alliance with big business boosted him to victory; America's millionaires uncorked the champagne when he defeated Harrison. His campaign's pact to sell influence wasn't without its price, however. The cozy deals on tariffs later caused the two-time president humiliation when one of his cabinet officials, Secretary of War Daniel Lamont, was accused of using inside information to reap a huge profit on the sugar tariff.

"It could probably be shown by the facts and figures that there is no distinctly native American criminal class except Congress."

—MARK TWAIN

CORTELYOUISM

One of Teddy Roosevelt's well-intentioned ideas blew up in his face during the 1904 election. The trust-busting "T.R." loathed the unbridled influence that the big corporations wielded at the turn of the century. During the first year of his presidency, according to one estimate in *Arena* magazine, one-eighth of the population owned seven-eighths of the nation's growing wealth; more significantly, one percent of rich industrialists controlled fifty-four percent of the U.S. resources. The reformist Roosevelt had created a special Bureau of Corporations within the Department of Commerce to gather information on the big corporations.

However, when he ran as an incumbent in 1904, Roosevelt chose his Secretary of Commerce, George Cortelyou, as his national campaign manager. T.R.'s attempt to keep an eye on the huge conglomerates backfired when Cortelyou began hustling six-figure donations from corporations under his department's jurisdiction. "Cortelyouism" became synonymous with the cabinet chief's heavy-handed style of soliciting campaign funds.

"Buying the President," blared an editorial in the *New York Times*. Especially galling to Roosevelt was a $100,000 gift to his party from Standard Oil, a company he'd clashed with repeatedly. The president claimed persuasively not to know about the donation and ordered it returned. However, it was later revealed that big business had given the then-astonishing sum of a million dollars to Roosevelt's Republicans, more than the corporate moguls had contributed to the Democrats.

When the dust cleared and he was reelected, Roosevelt asked Congress to prohibit all corporate contributions.

VOTER AUCTION

He may have been the most feared muckraker of his day, but journalist Lincoln Steffens's crusading reputation didn't stop the local politicians near his residence in Greenwich, Connecticut, from buying votes as usual. Even this accepted form of corruption wasn't equitable, however. In his autobiography, Steffens noted that Yankee voters in his community were paid $2.50 for their votes, but Italians typically got $2.75.

RAGTIME POLITICS

Does this sound like a typical visit to a polling place? "There were as yet no voting machines. The voter stepped gingerly into a curtained-off space, sat down at a rickety table, and with heart in mouth, marked his vote on the ballot with a pencil. His heart was in his mouth because there was always a likelihood that a hefty 'election watcher' might dart in and catch him voting for the wrong side."

This was ragtime-era politics in Chicago, as described by reporter Ben Hecht, the colorful journalist who was the role model for the play and movie *The Front Page*. The poll monitors, asserted Hecht, were there to make sure the voter was not "unduly influenced" by common practices of "free liquor, a free flop, a free lunch in the saloon, a patronage appointment, or when flattery failed . . . assault and battery. Most of the election judges were ruffians wearing badges."

In the Roaring Twenties, votes also were stolen by so-called "short pencil men," who palmed pencil stubs as they counted vote tallies and subtly defaced opposition ballots so they wouldn't count, according to Chicago writers Bill and Lori Granger.

"A day or two before the election," wrote Hecht, "the vital wards of the town filled up with hordes of drunks, hopheads and bearded hoboes" eager for free booze, prostitutes, and voting bonuses of several dollars each.

COVERING UP CARRIE

The stern, moralizing bosses of the Republican party's Old Guard successfully bribed their way out of a possible sex scandal before the 1920 presidential election. Their candidate, Ohio senator Warren Harding, was a handsome, genial politician whose greatest goal in life was to be liked by everyone with whom he came into contact. His fondness for young, nubile females continued long after his marriage to his ambitious, aristocratic wife Florence, whose imperious personality earned her the nickname "The Duchess."

One of Harding's longer-lasting affairs was with the thirtyish Carrie Phillips, the wife of a close friend. Their liaison lasted five years, and prompted gushing letters of affection and undying devotion from Harding, some of them running more than thirty pages in length. The secret romance broke up only when Carrie moved away and Harding decided that divorce might destroy his political future.

After the Ohio senator was unexpectedly nominated to run for the presidency, however, his political handlers sensed possible scandal, although the former lovers had not been in touch for several years. Carrie Phillips could not be allowed to become a public embarrassment, or a threat to their nominee's chances to capture the White House.

One of Harding's men was quietly sent to Carrie with an attractive bribe: she would be given $20,000 in cash, plus an all-expenses paid trip abroad with her husband, if she would agree to stay out of the country until the election was over. Apparently over her years-long obsession with the doting, middle-aged senator, she agreed without hesitation.

The preelection payoff didn't stifle Harding's overactive hormones, though; long before the Republican errand boys covered up his affair with Carrie, he'd become involved with the much younger Nan Britton, who'd worshiped Harding from afar as a teenager. Their years-long affair lasted throughout Harding's presidency. Nan claimed Harding was the father of a child born the year before the election; he supported the child and continued to communicate with her through a trusted Secret Service agent while in the White House.

CAUTIOUS CAL'S SECRET DEAL

In 1824, General Andy Jackson's loyalists charged that a "corrupt bargain" by John Q. Adams, designed to solicit additional political backing, cheated their hero out of the presidency. Exactly one hundred years later, rumors swirled around the 1924 presidential campaign that the reticent, calculating Calvin Coolidge made a similar, secret deal for auto magnate Henry Ford's support.

Actually, under different circumstances, the genius inventor might have been elected president himself in 1924. He was the most popular public figure in the Midwest region and far western states. Ford's fame, including his well-publicized views against war profiteers and in favor of better conditions for workers, made him a formidable potential candidate.

In an article for *Colliers* magazine entitled, "If I Were President," Ford denounced "the evils of railroad management." On a more disturbing note, noted Ford biographer Keith Seward, he also blasted "Jew financiers" who he claimed were behind the labor union organizing efforts he detested. Despite his anti-Semitism, a *Colliers* opinion poll showed him the overwhelming choice of voters, even when matched against accomplished public servants such as Herbert Hoover.

Nevertheless, there was something Henry Ford wanted more than to live in the White House—he lusted for control of power sites and nitrate plants in the Tennessee Valley, which Congress previously had built up as a war measure. A man of grandiose vision, Ford's fondest dreams were centered on immense reserves of resources and land in an area called Muscle Shoals,

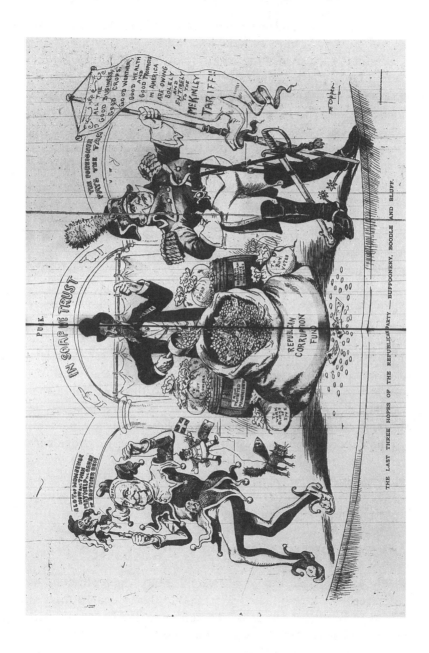

which would come under the management of the Tennessee Valley Authority (TVA) a decade later.

Aching to gain ownership of the sprawling public tract, Ford made a self-serving financial proposition to the federal government to lease the rights to the Wilson Dam on the property for a hundred years. The long-term proposal, part of a larger package that would have earned Ford an untold fortune, at no risk to his own holdings, captivated many congressmen with its promise of untapped water power. But it was denounced as a raw deal for the taxpayers by Ford's detractors, who felt the industrialist's unconventional views made him unfit for the highest office.

In December 1923, when he was still one of the leading possible candidates for president, Ford met privately with President Coolidge, who'd become the nation's chief executive after Warren Harding unexpectedly died the previous August. Not long afterward, in a message to Congress that didn't mention Ford by name, Coolidge recommended the sale of Muscle Shoals to private interests.

When Ford later endorsed Coolidge ("I would never for a moment think of running against Calvin Coolidge for President on any ticket"), newspaper editorialists and at least one participant in the White House meeting came to the conclusion that "Silent Cal" and Ford had struck an implicit bargain—Muscle Shoals in return for the automaker's withdrawal as a candidate.

Whether or not they cooked up a backroom plot, Coolidge won election and remained in the White House for four more years. But Ford never got title to the coveted Tennessee Valley lands; his attempted acquisition was blocked by determined opposition in the Senate, and he finally gave up his cherished dream.

THE PUBLIC-MINDED "SCARFACE"

No doubt in a gesture of civic responsibility, mob chieftan Al "Scarface" Capone donated $250,000 to the campaign fund of Chicago's William "Big Bill" Thompson in 1927. The quarter-million-dollar windfall certainly increased Mr. Capone's "access" to certain city officials.

FDR'S SECRET TAPES

Irritated at what he considered misleading embellishments of his private comments to members of Congress in Oval Office meetings, Franklin D. Roosevelt ordered his stenographer, Henry Kannee, to find a method of accurately recording White House discussions. After failing to find a satisfactory solution with a dictaphone, FDR was provided in 1940 with one of the first operational sound recording machines, which recorded sound on film stock; the microphone was placed either in his desk lamp or a drawer.

Portions of the recordings, retrieved forty years later by Professor R.T.C. Butow and Marc Weiss, show the more Machiavellian, political side of Roosevelt, and reveal his concern that Republican opponent Wendell Willkie might have devastating campaign material to unleash against him.

The Willkie campaign had obtained letters written by Roosevelt's running mate, Agriculture Secretary Henry Wallace, to a Russian mystic that were headed by the salutation "Dear Guru." Wallace already was considered an oddball by many, and no doubt the letters would be leaked by Willkie loyalists to ridicule the Democratic ticket.

FDR decided to take active measures to ensure that Wallace's ill-advised correspondence remained private, at least until the election was over. The wily politician knew that his opponent Willkie had his own Achilles' heel; it was common knowledge among political insiders that he was estranged from his wife and had a mistress in New York.

According to the transcripts of an August 1940 conversation with aide Lowell Mellett, the president concluded that the rumored marital infidelity could be used against Willkie: "We can spread it as a word-of-mouth thing, or by some people, way, way down the line. We can't have any of our principal speakers refer to it, but the people down the line can get it out."

Slamming the desk to reinforce his point, Roosevelt continued: "I mean the Congress speakers, the state speakers, and so forth, *they* can use the raw material . . . *Now, now,* if they want to play dirty politics in the end, we've got our own people . . . Now you'd be amazed at how this story about the gal is spreading around the country . . ."

"It's out," Mellett interjected.

"Awful nice gal," Roosevelt observed drily. "Writes for the magazine and so forth and so on, a book reviewer. But nevertheless, there is the *fact*. And one very good way of bringing it out is by calling attention to the *parallel* in conversation . . ."

The "parallel" Roosevelt was referring to was a situation that involved his fellow New York politician, "Gentleman" Jimmy Walker, the mayor of New York. The dandified Walker had been living openly with a woman, "an extremely attractive little tart," according to Roosevelt's recorded description, during a time when Walker had separated from his wife.

Despite keeping his girlfriend on the side, Walker audaciously paid his estranged spouse to make a public appearance with him in Albany at a time when he and his Tammany Hall administration associates were on trial for corruption before none other than Roosevelt, who as governor was in charge of the state investigation.

"Jimmy had never spent a Sunday in Albany in his life, but Mrs. Walker comes up to Albany, lives with him, ostensibly at the same suite in the hotel, and on Sunday the two of them go to Mass at the Albany Cathedral together. Price? *Ten thousand dollars!*

"Mrs. Willkie may not have been hired" to make campaign appearances, FDR conceded while drawing a comparison, "but in effect she's been hired to return to Wendell and smile and make this campaign with him. Now, whether there was a money price behind it, I don't know, but it's the same idea . . ."

Neither the Wallace letters nor the allegations about Mrs. Willkie surfaced as public issues during the 1940 presidential campaign, which resulted in a third term for the resourceful Roosevelt.

LANDSLIDE LYNDON

The 1948 U.S. Senate Democratic primary in Texas was "the beginning of modern politics," as John Connally, one of the state's favorite sons, has said with only a bit of overstatement. Representing Lyndon Johnson's last-gasp chance at winning national office, the bitter, incredibly intense primary battle between him and former governor Coke Stevenson was the first big-money election race in the Lone Star State's history. The two main combatants presented a stark contrast, both in the way they campaigned and the lengths to which each would go to win. Most significantly, it was almost undoubtedly a stolen election; one in which a scant eighty-seven disputed votes gave LBJ his nickname of "Landslide Lyndon" and propelled him toward the White House.

As Johnson's biographer Robert Caro has painstakingly documented, LBJ's desperate effort to defeat the well-regarded Stevenson revolutionized modern politics in several ways: he became probably the first candidate to utilize a helicopter, dubbed the "Johnson City Windmill" by reporters, to transport him and his inimitable, personal style of campaigning throughout the vast expanses of rural Texas. When the airborne assault didn't significantly cut Stevenson's lead in the polls, however, Johnson made unprecedented use of radio as an additional campaign tool and resorted to more familiar tactics: he set out to destroy the upright reputation of Stevenson, known as "Mr. Texas," who is portrayed by Caro as a sort of Diogenes on horseback—the last of the plainspoken, incorruptible frontiersmen.

Opening up by painting Stevenson as indecisive, Johnson attacked him as "Mr. Straddler," and "Mr. Do-Nothinger." That was just a warm-up. Lying about his wartime service, LBJ claimed to have engaged in combat in the Pacific when instead he had used his official connections and connived to obtain a safe state-side job visiting navy contractors on the West Coast for most of the war.

Johnson also falsely charged that Stevenson would act to repeal the crucial Taft-Hartley labor legislation if elected, and then tried to brand the conservative rancher as a Communist for failing to publicly state his position on the law. COMMUNISTS FAVOR COKE blared one headline in a rural newspaper, an attack that made an impression on Texas farmers who had no idea about Stevenson's position on unions.

None of the ugly campaign invective was enough to enable the increasingly nervous Johnson to catch up to the more popular Stevenson, who steadfastly (and probably foolishly) refused to get down in the dirt with his determined opponent. More drastic measures needed to be taken, and Johnson never hesitated. In many south Texas counties, where dollars meant votes, ballots were bought, changed, miscounted and even forged to close the gap in the polls. Developers who'd tied their financial fortunes to Johnson's political future dumped hundreds of thousands of dollars in cash around the state to save their man's influence in Washington. In one county, an unlikely total of 99.6 percent of the citizens listed on the poll tax registry voted—in an area with a large illiteracy rate. Johnson got more than 98 percent of these votes.

When the highly questionable final tally showed Johnson the statewide winner by a mere eighty-seven votes, he had to survive an executive committee investigation by his own party (the minority report charged him with "palpable fraud and irregularities," a document he and his supporters blithely ignored). Outflanking Democrats squeamish about certifying his controversial candidacy, Johnson promised to seat pro-Truman delegates at the 1948 state convention to quell a potential party rebellion. "Landslide Lyndon" also beat back several court challenges by Stevenson and his outraged backers with the backstage help of the brilliant lawyer Abe Fortas, who was later rewarded for his assistance with a seat on the Supreme Court.

In 1977, Luis Salas, the election judge of Duval County, which had virtually handed the primary victory to LBJ by "reporting" 200 pro-Johnson votes in "Box 13" *after* the polls had closed, confessed the outcome had been rigged. Furthermore, he asserted, Johnson had been present at a meeting when the plans were made. "If they [the votes] were not for Johnson, I made them for Johnson,'' he admitted, thirty years after the theft.

The general election was a cakewalk compared to the life-and-death struggle for the nomination; Johnson easily defeated Republican Jack Porter and soon became a power broker among Washington Democrats.

Coke Stevenson retired from active politics to his ranch, married a much younger woman, and lived to the age of eighty-seven.

THE MOB'S MESSENGER

Oddly, one of Richard Nixon's most noble moments might have come at the occasion of a bitter political defeat—his closely contested loss to John F. Kennedy in the 1960 presidential election. Nixon's Republican supporters were livid at Kennedy's razor-thin margin of victory in several key states, and claimed, not without cause, that the election might have been stolen by fraud and voting irregularities, especially in Illinois and Texas.

Recounting the vote, however, would have proven a daunting task. As Nixon himself later admitted, ''it would take at least a year and half to get a recount in Cook County [Chicago], and . . . there was no procedure whatever for a recount in Texas.'' To his credit, Nixon refused to demand such a recount, knowing it would throw the nation into an ugly, protracted political struggle, and in Nixon's words, would ''downgrade democracy.'' Nevertheless, he privately remarked that ''we won but they stole it from us.''

Nixon may have had more reason to complain than even he knew at the time. There were widespread rumors that the Kennedy family fortune found its way into voting districts in the swing states of Illinois and West Virginia, and that he would not have been either the Democratic nominee or the winning candidate without the immense power of the Kennedy family fortune.

More than thirty years after the election, Judith Campbell Exner, a self-proclaimed former girlfriend of the late president,

asserted that JFK made her a courier for deliveries of money to the late Chicago crime boss Sam Giancana. She insisted she was involved sexually with both men. The first delivery of cash, which she said was intended for Giancana's henchmen to distribute in exchange for votes, was given to her in early April 1960, after a dinner during which the crucial West Virginia primary election was discussed.

While Kennedy's retainers made substantial, legal contributions to local West Virginia politicians, they covered their bets with other, less savory donations, according to Exner's account. One of Giancana's associates, "Skinny" D'Amato, is quoted by writer Anthony Summers as saying that the mob chieftan sent him to West Virginia "to get votes for Jack Kennedy." Kennedy won the critical primary and went on to victory in Illinois in the general election as a result of highly disputed votes in Cook County, where Giancana and Democratic mayor Richard Daley presided over their own separate fiefdoms.

While no one knows the full details of the alleged Kennedy connection to the vicious Giancana, Exner provided writers with personal records and appointment logs backing her link to Kennedy. It's also now a matter of record that federal law enforcement authorities, including the FBI, later went into a panic about the Kennedy-Exner relationship, and her association with the feared Giancana, who was later murdered in an organized crime power struggle.

The 1960 election might have hinged on some purchased votes and the electoral legwork of a notorious Mafia boss, who fervently believed that Kennedy had double-crossed him and reneged on unspoken bargains after the votes were bought.

TALL TALES FROM TEXAS

Lynson Johnson loved to chew the political fat with his friends in Congress over a scotch or two; and his tall tales, whether true or more likely embellished for dramatic effect, fascinated his Capitol Hill audiences. According to former House Doorkeeper

William "Fishbait" Miller, LBJ's favorite stories were about illegal voting, even when they involved him.

One of the most frequently told involved a man who came to see him for a favor, and who unhesitatingly pointed out that he deserved Senator Johnson's assistance, as he had voted faithfully for LBJ in all his House and Senate races in Texas.

As Johnson related in his Hill County accent, "So naturally, Ah thanked the man foh his fine support and Ah said, 'Mah friend, what can Ah do for you?'

"Mah visitor said, 'Well, Senator, after all Ah did to help you, Ah wonder if you could help me become a citizen?' "

Another LBJ cocktail hour story passed on by Fishbait involved two Texas fellows who were copying names from tombstones just before an election. When they came to a grave marker that was so old and worn that they couldn't read the name, one of the collaborators suggested moving on, but the other stubbornly kept trying to decipher it.

"What's the matter with you," said the one in a hurry. "Why are you staying here?"

"Well, Ah care," said the other one. "This man's got every bit as much right to vote as all the rest of these fellows here."

THAT WAS IN THE OFF-SEASON

The blustery shipping executive George Steinbrenner, ex-owner of the New York Yankees baseball team, was convicted in 1974 of violating federal campaign contribution laws relating to a six-figure gift to Richard Nixon's 1972 presidential campaign. To hear former House Speaker Thomas "Tip" O'Neill tell the story, though, the controversial Steinbrenner was virtually blackmailed into breaking the law by Nixon's greedy fund-raisers at the infamous Committee to Re-Elect the President (CREEP).

After Steinbrenner quit the Republican party and began giving hefty donations to the Democrats, he and the Massachusetts congressman became buddies, often going to Boston Red Sox–Yankees' games together. In 1972, however, O'Neill related that

he became concerned when the wealthy Steinbrenner failed to
ante up his usual generous contribution to the Democratic party.
"What's the matter," O'Neill asked the sports magnate.
"Why don't I hear from you anymore?"

"I've got a problem," Steinbrenner confided to the burly Irish
politician. "They're holding the hammer over my head."

"They," as it turned out, were Nixon aides unhappy that the
party-switching Steinbrenner wasn't giving any money to the
Republicans. According to O'Neill, after Steinbrenner refused to
head up a "Democrats for Nixon" committee, the president's
fund-raisers asked for a large campaign contribution as an alternative. They also hinted to Steinbrenner that government investigations pending against his companies at the Justice and Labor
departments might recede, if he put a substantial gift in CREEP's
bulging coffers.

"I'm a Democrat," Steinbrenner told Nixon's emissaries. "I'll
give you twenty-five thou" ($25,000). Not enough, responded
CREEP fund-raiser and Nixon lawyer Herbert Kalmbach, who
made it clear that he wanted $100,000. To get around the legal
campaign contribution limits, Kalmbach further suggested that
Steinbrenner write thirty-three separate checks for $3,000 and
one last check for $1,000.

Steinbrenner gave in to what amounted to a shakedown, and
concealed the contributions by awarding bonuses to his corporate
employees, who were then asked to turn the extra money over to
the Nixon campaign.

As a result of the subsequent conviction, baseball commissioner Bowie Kuhn suspended Steinbrenner from the sport for
two years. Irate over the harsh penalty, Steinbrenner's lawyer,
Edward Bennett Williams, asked Kuhn why he hadn't similarly
suspended Houston Astros' outfielder Cesar Cedeno, who'd been
convicted of involuntary manslaughter. "That was different,"
the commissioner replied. "Cedeno did that in the off-season."

TELL THEM YOU GAVE AT THE OFFICE

Spiro Agnew resigned the vice-presidency in October 1973 after pleading *nolo contendere,* or "no contest," to evading federal tax on unreported income he received while governor of Maryland. Federal prosecutors learned that Agnew believed that it was customary for engineers to receive no-bid contracts from the state to make payments to the governor. The investigation showed that Agnew demanded and got such payments even before he became governor, while serving as executive for Baltimore County, and that he continued to take them even after becoming vice-president of the United States.

Agnew wasn't without a sense of humor about the payoff system, however. One engineer, Lester Matz, had previously given Agnew thousands of dollars in cash in conjunction with Maryland contracts, and later provided Agnew with $2,500 for help in securing a federal contract. When Matz was strong-armed for a political donation by the Nixon-Agnew election campaign of 1972, the vice-presidential nominee quipped to his friend: "Tell them you gave at the office."

MR. AFRICA

The voters of Michigan seem to be a forgiving bunch. The state's first elected black congressman, Charles Diggs, became a powerful voice for minority interests on Capitol Hill. He was even dubbed "Mr. Africa" by his colleagues because of his expertise on the continent's people and politics. Unfortunately, Rep. Diggs also had a well-developed taste for the good life; and with three marriages, six children, and a bankrupt family funeral business, he didn't have the means to support his expensive habits.

Congressman Diggs decided to resolve his financial woes by giving his staffers huge raises, and then forcing them to kick back up to two-thirds of their salaries to pay his over-extended living expenses. He also generously paid personal employees, such as his lawyer and accountant, with federal funds, although they had no government jobs and were not on the public payroll. Convicted on twenty-nine counts of federal mail fraud and taking kickbacks from his staff, Diggs was sentenced to three years in prison in October 1978 and agreed to make himself scarce during the final days of the 95th Congress.

The next month he was easily reelected.

THIS IS IT?

Campaign contributions have been made in some unusual places, but probably none stranger than "This Is It," a bawdy striptease joint located in Washington, D.C.'s Fourteenth Street red-light district. During the Christmas season of 1981, Mayor Marion Barry's limousine was parked outside the establishment, where "ladies dance around in nothing but their dimples," in the words of a newspaper columnist.

Hizzoner, of course, wasn't there to ogle the club's exotic performers. "I have good vision and good eyes," said the mayor, "and I didn't see any naked women there." Rather, the holiday season soiree at "This Is It" was a "formal affair," Barry stated. He had merely dropped by to solicit or pick up campaign contributions, according to what he told the city's chief of police and others.

Evidently the mayor had some extra time after taking care of the evening's political agenda: witnesses inside the club told reporters and police officials that Barry snorted cocaine and sought sexual favors from female employees at the party. "The stories were true," the owner of the nightclub later revealed to a local television station. "He's a pretty blatant fellow."

Dubbed "Mayor For Life" by one political wag, Barry denied the drug and sex allegations and stuck by his campaign contributions cover story. Almost a decade later, however, he was arrested by federal agents who had videotaped him consuming cocaine with a girlfriend recruited by the FBI to snare him in an undercover sting operation.

"The bitch set me up," was the mayor's explanation for that episode, which at least temporarily derailed his political career.

RUN FOR OFFICE—OR ELSE

The recruiting of political candidates gets a little rough in South Dakota. Perhaps a bit over-anxious to field a formidable Republican challenger to run against Senator Tom Daschle (D) in 1992, the state's GOP strategists tried, in their words, to "entice" former governor Bill Janklow to throw his hat into the ring. Their ten-page plan to "draft" Janklow, however, sounded more like a plot to strong-arm him into entering the race than a polite request to one of the party faithful.

The plan began by predicting dire consequences should Janklow refuse to face Daschle: "Bill Janklow risks his future political career by not accepting the draft." The ex-governor's admirers also wanted to organize a "party celebrating a Janklow friend and legal advisor's recovery from cancer to elicit an emotional endorsement of the draft Janklow effort."

Other details called for a "letter from [President George] Bush, to be published in the *Argus Leader* and *Rapid City Journal,* on the anniversary of the Persian Gulf air war, saying 'Bill, your country needs you.' " The activists also wanted Bush to call their man personally and press him to run.

State Democratic officials termed the proposal "a cynical and manipulative document." One legislator labeled it "blackmail." Even some GOP loyalists admitted that some parts of the plan were "unsavory," but shrugged it off as "politics as usual."

"It is a plan to smear Tom Daschle and threaten Bill Janklow," editorialized the *Rapid City Journal.*

THE LAST BANANA REPUBLIC

Politics doesn't get any stranger than the weird, hybrid mix of populism, corruption, and Cajun-flavored oddness that dominates Louisiana. The Bayou State, which produced the legendary demagogue and reformer Huey Long, may be "America's last banana republic," according to one of the state's top political analysts, John Maginnis.

Those who doubt that description need only take a cursory look at the state's last gubernatorial election. Former three-time governor Edwin Edwards, a charming, roguish populist in the Long tradition, was seeking yet another return to the governor's mansion. Popular during his first two terms in the 1970s, he was twice indicted for criminal acts and testified before federal grand juries no less than fifteen times during the third turn in office. After a hung jury ended his first trial, he was acquitted in the second, but widely regarded as politically terminal.

"People like to boast about how honest they are. I've got all kinds of pieces of paper to prove it. I've been through sixteen grand juries," he was quoted as saying in the *Wall Street Journal*. In most states, of course, repeated visits to the grand jury room wouldn't be a welcome addition to a political résumé.

One of the most notorious ladies' men in Southern politics, Edwards reveled in, rather than hid, his decades-long reputation for amorous conquests. Advisers' efforts to subdue his rakish image were unraveled by the sixty-four-year-old divorcé's campaign appearances with his twenty-six-year-old girlfriend, Candy.

Meanwhile, the Republican side of the ledger had its own rather unique cast of characters. Handsome, telegenic, articulate, forty-one-year-old David Duke looked every bit the part of a potential GOP standard-bearer. A former member of the racist Ku Klux Klan ("I never wore a hood, but I wore a robe"), he quit the KKK in 1980 to form his own hate organization, the National Association for the Advancement of White People (NAAWP). In addition, his enthusiastic selling of Nazi and anti-Semitic literature, up until two years before the governor's race, caused his chosen party and the Bush White House to disavow him. Nevertheless, the controversial Duke remained quite popular in sections of the state where 1892 is a more popular date than 1992.

Caught between the other two "mainstream" candidates was the sitting governor, former congressman Buddy Roemer. Although a Democrat while serving in Washington, he delighted the Bush White House by defecting to the Republicans in 1990. At first glance, the hardworking, rather uptight Roemer appeared like a choirboy compared to his two more colorful rivals.

Buddy had his own quirks, however: whenever a negative thought came into the governor's mind, for instance, he snapped a rubber band worn around his wrist and muttered, "Cancel. Cancel." His favorite book at the time of the campaign was *All I Really Needed to Know I Learned in Kindergarten*. A Roemer afternoon of excitement was reading a book while attending a New Orleans Saints football game, where the more ardent fans used to be known for wearing paper bags over their heads during their team's leaner years.

The honest but uninspiring Buddy finished a dismal third in the primary balloting, which left the Louisiana voters with an unappetizing choice between a former Nazi and the lovable rogue, Edwards, who a federal prosecutor once accused of having two million dollars in gambling debts. Fear of Duke was so rampant that some of Edwards's most bitter enemies offered their support. Voters in the state Hollywood called "The Big Easy" (and the *Washington Post* called "The Big Sleazy"), held their noses and sent the well-worn Edwards back to the governor's residence for a fourth time.

Maybe Huey Long wasn't so bad after all.

RETIRING IN STYLE

Approximately one-third of the members of the House of Representatives could pocket as much as $41 million in leftover campaign money for personal use, if they leave office by the end of 1992, states a report by the Center for Public Integrity. Two senior congressmen, Stephen Solarz of New York and Dan Rostenkowski of Illinois, chairman of the powerful House Ways and Means Committee, have amassed more than a million dollars each in leftover campaign funds, which could be turned into lucrative "golden parachutes" for their retirements. At least seventeen other members have more than $500,000 in their private war chests.

Although Congress passed a law in 1980 to prohibit legislators from keeping unused campaign money, a glaring loophole exempted members who were in office before January 1980. The result was a bonanza for departing representatives such as California Republican Robert Badham, who spent $40,000 in leftover campaign funds for such goodies as formal wear, jewelry for his wife, club dues, and dry cleaning. Another Republican, Gene Taylor of Missouri, exited Capitol Hill with $345,000 for his personal use, and the family of the late Tennessee congressman John Duncan got $605,000 from his campaign coffers.

Dozens of congressmen eligible to take advantage of the leftover goodies have announced that they won't leave Congress by the legal deadline, or won't take the windfall if they do. But legally, nothing can stop them from cashing in if they change their minds, and many others have made no commitment.

SMOKE-FILLED ROOMS

A POLITICAL ART FORM

Gerrymandering is the delicate art of altering the configuration of a voting district so that while one party has a majority in a large number of districts, the other side's strength is concentrated in as few districts as possible.

The term originated with Massachusetts governor Elbridge Gerry, who in 1812 devised a district that critics said was shaped like a salamander: similar attempts at drawing weird electoral boundaries in order to confound the opposition thereafter were known as gerrymanders. The practice is still popular as a tool for protecting congressional or state legislative incumbents whose seats are threatened by population shifts, or changes in the ethnic or party preference of their district.

THE CORRUPT BARGAIN

The hotly contested presidential election of 1824 produced a split result that threw the final decision to the House of Representatives. Although several candidates had received electoral votes, the two crucial remaining contenders were the New England son of a former president, John Quincy Adams, and the "Old Hero," the military legend General Andrew Jackson. Their showdown had been preceded by months of shadowy backroom wheeling and dealing. Despite winning a plurality of both popular and electoral votes in the general election, Jackson was defeated by Adams's bare majority of state electoral ballots in the House runoff.

To his credit, the fiery-tempered Jackson, who had been in more than one armed duel of honor, initially took the agonizing setback in a gentlemanly fashion. Soon afterward, however, Adams made an appointment that was either a harebrained decision or a political payoff—he made Henry Clay his administration's secretary of state. Clay, who had contended for the presidency himself, was abhorred by his rival Jackson.

The outraged Jacksonian backers howled that a "corrupt bar-gain" had been struck between Adams and Clay *before* the election, and that the unethical collusion had cheated their beloved soldier-hero out of a victory he'd rightly won at the polls. Since Clay, who felt he should be president, couldn't win himself, he'd thrown his support behind Adams in exchange for a post that placed him closer to his real ambition, in the view of Jackson's disappointed supporters. "All the waters of the sweet Heavens cannot remove the iota of corruption," wrote one Clay critic.

No solid proof was produced to back the accusation, but none was necessary in the minds of Jackson and his unhappy partisans. While Adams had relatively little popular support in Kentucky, Ohio, and Missouri, their representatives had cast their state's electoral votes for Adams. "So you see," the defeated Jackson wrote bitterly, "the Judas of the West has closed the contract and will receive his thirty pieces of silver. His end will be the same."

The backers of South Carolina's John Calhoun, who'd originally been a candidate in the presidential race but instead had settled for being elected vice-president, jumped into the Jackson camp. They didn't like Clay, either. Swallowing what he considered an immoral deal between two political enemies, the Old Hero soon began putting together a nationwide political organization that would put him in the White House four years later, without benefit of another congressional tie-breaking vote.

TIPPECANOE AND A LOG CABIN, TOO?

While it's uncertain as to exactly when political image-shapers took over presidential campaigns, their commanding role unquestionably extends back to 1840. One of the most famous and effective election slogans of the nineteenth century was the rallying cry "Tippecanoe and Tyler, Too," referring to the Whig ticket of General William Henry Harrison, the hero of the Indian battle of Tippecanoe, and his running mate, John Tyler.

Since President Martin Van Buren had suffered through the

economic Panic of 1837 and had been dubbed "Martin Van Ruin" by his political opponents, Harrison's handlers had a simple blueprint for victory—muzzle Harrison and let his heroic reputation carry him into the White House.

His advisers, who included Major David Gwynne and Judge John C. Wright, kept their man on the short leash, and were labeled the "Conscience-Keeping Committee" by the Democrats. Their candidate was derisively called "General Mum" for his enforced silence. With the hovering members of the inner circle responding to much of the general's correspondence, rumors circulated that the sixty-eight-year-old Harrison was secretly infirm and unable to speak for himself; he finally was forced to attend a public rally to dispel the whispers.

But it wasn't just Harrison's coterie of manipulative protectors that infuriated the Democrats. The humble, log cabin origins attributed to the military hero, and energetically promoted by his supporters, sent opponents into paroxysms of rage. Harrison, charged a critic, "Is not a poor man, he does not live in a log cabin . . . He is a rich man, he lives in a magnificent frame house, is surrounded with a princely estate . . . So, sir, all this story about the log cabin is a falsehood. It is a mean fraud."

Meanwhile, Van Buren's backers responded by spreading malicious tales, including one that a Winnebago Indian squaw represented her three sons as Harrison's; and therefore the bastard children were deserving of substantial government annuities. According to the St. Louis *Daily Argus,* the illegitimate off-spring drew "about $1,000 apiece."

The aging Harrison grew weary of the nasty electoral broadsides, but he stayed out on the campaign stump longer than he'd intended, explaining:

I am here because I am the most persecuted and
calumniated individual now living; because I have been
slandered by reckless opponents to the extent that I am
devoid of every qualification, physical, mental and moral,
for the high place to which at least a respectable portion
of my fellow citizens have nominated me.

Harrison won the election handily, but his victory was short-lived. He apparently took his doctor's preelection assurance of good health too literally. Ignoring the freezing, blustery weather on his inauguration day and refusing to wear a coat, he fell ill and died within a month of his swearing-in, propelling the more controversial Tyler into the presidency.

"All Members of Congress have a primary interest in being reelected. Some members have no other interest."
—FORMER REPRESENTATIVE FRANK E. SMITH

A REAL DARK HORSE

The man who became perhaps America's greatest president wasn't a shoo-in for the office he first won in 1860. On the contrary, Abraham Lincoln (he hated the nickname "Abe") was a bit of a long shot to win the Republican nomination at the party's Chicago convention. Senator William H. Seward, who had the backing of an unscrupulous New York political boss with the evil-sounding name of Thurlow Weed, was the leading candidate when the head-counting started.

While many observers believed that Lincoln was the only politician who could unite various feuding factions of the Republican party, he might never have gotten the chance if it hadn't been for the clever backstage maneuvers of David Davis, one of his top managers. Davis imported thousands of Illinois Republicans into Chicago to campaign for "honest Abe," who was nowhere to be found. (He remained in Springfield awaiting the party's decision and expecting bad news.) Meanwhile, Davis was telling anyone who would listen that the Republican ticket would surely go down to defeat in the general election if headed by Seward, a man with a lot of political IOU's, but also many enemies.

The strategy to undermine Seward worked; his broad but shallow support cracked after he failed to take control on the second

ballot, and the lanky rail-splitter won an unexpected victory. He might later have wished he hadn't: in the South, Lincoln was burned in effigy, and his name didn't even appear on the ballot in ten Dixie states. Southern Democrats called the Republican nominee the greatest "ass" in the country, a "blood-thirsty tyrant" and a "horrid looking wrench" who would abolish slavery, give freed blacks all the federal government jobs, and urge them to copulate with the delicate white belles of the plantations.

Needless to say, the Great Emancipator didn't start out with the nation united behind his rather unlikely presidency.

ANYBODY BUT GRANT

If a campaign ever literally killed a presidential hopeful, the victim was Horace Greeley in 1872. A crusading editor who'd helped sway the 1860 Republican convention away from New York Senator William Seward and to Abraham Lincoln, Greeley found himself a dozen years later the somewhat surprising choice to try and thwart a reelection of Lincoln's successor, Ulysses S. Grant.

Greeley belonged to an influential foursome of Liberal Republican party editors called the "Quadrilaterals," whose sole platform was "anybody to beat Grant." While they never intended to make the bearded, bespectacled, potbellied Greeley their champion, fractious infighting among the other possible nominees resulted in a ground swell of support for the outspoken newspaperman. Not everyone was delighted. Another one of the "Quads," reformer Carl Schurz, complained that the Greeley nomination had been the outcome of a "successful piece of political hucksterism" by his fellow editor's backers.

Although it was a bitter pill to swallow, for Greeley had never voted Democratic and had previously denounced the party for its connection to the corrupt Tammany political machine, the Democratic faithful held their noses and also endorsed the editor, knowing that otherwise they faced almost certain defeat at the hands of Grant's Republicans. Nicknamed Old White Coat for his ever-present greatcoat, Greeley called for a "New Departure'' from the corruption and spoils system, which had flourished under Grant.

The campaign theme didn't impress the famous cartoonist Thomas Nast, who ferociously attacked Greeley, portraying him as catering to Tammany's Boss Tweed and being swallowed by a figure representing the racist Ku Klux Klan. Nast also lampooned Greeley's association with the party he formerly disdained by caricaturing him as a Scrooge-like figure eating from a steaming bowl labeled "My Own Words And Deeds.''

Business interests, rallying around Grant, pasted Greeley with a torrent of abuse, labeling him a secessionist and a slave trader, both ridiculous charges. They also claimed that if the editor became president, he would pay Confederate soldiers, retire the South's debt, and appoint former Confederates to his cabinet. His name was linked to radical feminists Victoria Woodhull and Tennessee Claflin, advocates of free love and equality for women. While the energetic journalist was praised as an inspiring orator by many of his contemporaries in the press, the *New York Times* sniffed: "If anyone could send a great nation to the dogs, the man is Greeley.''

The last weeks of the campaign were sheer torture for the besieged Greeley, who said that he was being assailed as though he were a candidate for the penitentiary instead of the presidency. After a long illness, his invalid wife died during the campaign. Meanwhile, his own fading health and the incessant pounding he was taking from political enemies caused him to write, in a letter to a friend two days before the election, ''I am not dead but I wish I were.''

Sick with ''brain fever'' and sinking into a morose mental state after losing to Grant by a significant margin, Greeley retreated to a hospital near his farm and died less than a month after the election. Because of his sudden death, his electoral votes were split up among other candidates.

IT'S WHO COUNTS THEM THAT MATTERS

During the 1870s heyday of Boss Tweed and his merry band of Tammany Hall thieves, elections were held—but they often meant nothing, as the outcome was preordained when the notorious New York patronage machine wanted their candidate in a particular office. That fact was confirmed years later by the corpulent Tweed himself, during a lengthy investigation into the Tammany Hall ring.

Question: "What were they [Tammany Hall] to do, in case you wanted a particular man elected over another?

Tweed: Count the ballots in bulk, or without counting them, announce the result in bulk, or change from one to the other, as the case may have been.

Question: Then these elections really were no elections at all? The ballots were made to bring about any result that you determined upon beforehand?

Tweed: The ballots made no result; the counters made the result.''

RUTHERFRAUD

Harry Truman wasn't the only chief executive to be prematurely and wrongly declared a presidential election loser. The first time it happened, in 1876, the razor-thin margin between victory and defeat threatened an armed insurrection over who should rightfully assume residence in the White House.

It was almost certainly a stolen election. The Republicans used wholesale fraud in a successful attempt to tip the balance in favor of their candidate, Ohio's Rutherford B. Hayes. When they belatedly saw the rug being unscrupulously pulled out from under their candidate, the Democrats employed brutal intimidation tactics in a last-ditch effort to salvage critical electoral votes for the man they thought had already won, New York governor Samuel Tilden.

Governor Hayes, a former congressman and Civil War hero, won slightly fewer popular votes (about a quarter million out of more than 8.3 million cast) than the capable but coldly calculating Tilden. Initially, the Democrats were correctly convinced on the basis of early returns that their man had won a close race; newspapers partial to Tilden claimed his victory the morning after the vote. An editorial in the *Indianapolis Journal* described the Democrats' anticipated celebration: "It was intoxicating in its effects, and operated on the Democratic system like a dose of hashish on a cultivated Hindoo stomach."

By the next morning, though, the Republican vote counters had calculated that Hayes could still win in the electoral college by one vote, *if* he carried all the electoral ballots of several southern states, such as Florida and Louisiana, where the final popular vote tally remained in doubt. When the shocked Democrats emerged from their stupor of self-congratulation and realized the final verdict was yet hanging in the balance, an all-out political war broke out over the returns from the few states that held the identity of the next president in their ballot boxes.

To ensure that Florida's electoral votes stayed in their camp, the Democrats employed a variation on the "Mississippi Plan" of intimidation against black voters, according to the detailed account of writer Paul Leland Haworth. Armed men showed up at Republican meetings, including one heckler who kept interrupting a black speaker with the challenge, "How many chickens have you stolen?" Other blacks were threatened with death if they joined Republican organizations. For their part, the GOP's voter-grabbers pulled just as many dirty stunts.

The Democratic campaign's goon squads were more circumspect in their dealings with an election canvassing board made up of distinguished politicians from outside the state; they unsuccessfully tried to bribe a couple of them. Fraud was committed by both sides in the count and return of votes in Florida and Louisiana. Perhaps well aware of the Democrats' willingness to buy the presidency if necessary, Louisiana's voting supervisors let it be known they would be amenable to delivering their state's key votes to Tilden—for a million dollars: but for some reason the proposition wasn't accepted.

As the controversy dragged on unresolved for more than a month, and it became more likely that Hayes, not Tilden, might emerge the eventual winner, the Democrats' mood understandably grew ugly. "Tilden or blood" was an ominous slogan heard in many corners. In the Midwest, Tilden "minutemen" were organized by former soldiers convinced that armed force might be necessary to settle the election stalemate. President Grant sent federal troops into the states with disputed votes, and some suggested that if the dispute couldn't be peacefully solved, he might have to remain in office temporarily.

Finally, almost in desperation, an electoral commission was formed by Congress to formally count the votes and declare, once and for all, who would be the next president. The Democrats pushed the idea as a last resort, but lost enthusiasm when they realized that the makeup of the bipartisan commission's members would likely dictate a vote in favor of Republican interests by a thin majority of 8–7 on almost every important issue. But by then they were stuck. Sensing a golden opportunity, politicians from the southern states who held Hayes's future tried to broker an unprecedented deal for a ticket to the White House—they'd support Hayes if he would agree to withdraw federal troops and permit greater autonomy in their state governments.

When a vote of both houses of Congress officially declared that Hayes had been elected president by awarding him all the disputed electoral votes, despite the fact that Tilden's ticket had clearly garnered more popular votes, the principled Ohio governor was denounced as a "Usurper," the "Boss Thief," and even "Rutherfraud." Even months later, after a trip to Europe to cool off, Tilden declared, not without cause, that he'd been cheated of the presidency by a "political crime."

More than a year later, however, the Democrats choked on their bitter words when it was disclosed that their party leaders had sent out carefully coded telegrams discussing bribery of election board members who controlled votes in the swing states. No solid proof was offered that Tilden knew of the plot, but it ended his intention to run again in 1880 to "right the great wrong" he'd suffered.

OUR MODERN BELSHAZZAR.

THE PEOPLE'S HANDWRITING ON THE WALL.

Hayes's successor in the White House, in fact, would be a Republican member of the controversial congressional commission, James Garfield.

"It is a choice between evils and I am going to shut my eyes, hold my nose, vote, go home and disinfect myself."
—TWO-TIME PRESIDENT GROVER CLEVELAND, DESCRIBING THE 1900 ELECTION BETWEEN FELLOW DEMOCRAT WILLIAM JENNINGS BRYAN AND REPUBLICAN WILLIAM McKINLEY. CLEVELAND REPORTEDLY VOTED FOR McKINLEY BECAUSE OF HIS DISTASTE FOR THE POPULIST BRYAN'S MONETARY POLICIES, WHICH INCLUDED ABANDONING THE GOLD STANDARD BELOVED BY BIG BUSINESS.

UNCLE EARL'S FLIP-FLOP

Political promises are often made to be broken, but few office-holders were as blunt about their mistakes as Louisiana's legendary governor, Earl Long. As his nephew, former senator Russell Long told the story, Uncle Earl once pledged during a campaign to let the voters of a particular area elect their own sheriff. After he won office, however, Earl tried to avoid a delegation who'd come to ask him to fulfill the commitment.

"I don't want to see 'em—you see 'em," Earl told an aide. "What'll I tell 'em?" asked the governor's factotum. "Tell 'em I lied," replied Earl candidly.

ACES FULL

The legend of the phrase "smoke-filled room" in American politics originated with the nomination of Warren Harding as the Republican party's candidate in the presidential election of 1920, according to several accounts. A newspaperman wrote that during an interview with Harding's friend and adviser Harry Daughtery, the shirt-sleeved politicians assembled were all sitting around puffing cigars.

The GOP's kingmakers must have practically suffocated from smoke inhalation by the conclusion of the sweltering, exhausting proceedings. Harding, then a well-liked but lightly regarded Ohio senator, wasn't anybody's first choice at the Chicago convention. In fact, one blunt political analyst said there *wasn't* any first choice: Harding was "the best of the second-raters." He was selected, in a late-developing ground swell, after several other, better-known hopefuls were rejected by party bosses and the delegates, who eventually turned to Harding. A well-dressed, affable politician with a distinguished appearance, he at least *looked* presidential, and could be counted on not to make any radical moves.

After ten rounds of frustrating balloting in the stifling heat, Harding finally emerged as the long-shot victor, as his mentor Daughtery had earlier predicted. The Republican nominee said jauntily, in the language of his cigar-chomping, poker-playing colleagues: "I feel like a man who goes in on a pair of eights and comes out with aces full." (However, other versions have quoted the pleasantly surprised candidate as saying, "We drew to a pair of deuces, and filled.")

THE KINGFISH'S BATTLE PLAN

Most of today's politicians won't go out on the hustings without the latest opinion poll, or a few highly paid consultants in tow. Huey Long had a much simpler campaign strategy. In 1923, during his first run for the Louisiana governorship, he confided his battle plan. "In every parish there is a boss, usually the sheriff. He has forty percent of the vote, forty percent are opposed to him, and twenty percent are the in-betweens. I'm going into every parish and cuss out the boss. That gives me forty percent to begin with, and I'll hoss trade 'em out of the in-betweens."

Despite this innovative strategy, however, the Louisiana Kingfish lost his first try for the state's top office in 1924.

"If you can't drink their booze, take their money, screw their women, and vote against them in the morning, you don't belong in this place."

> *"Money is the mother's milk of politics."*
> —CALIFORNIA ASSEMBLYMAN AND DEMOCRATIC POWER
> BROKER JESSE "BIG DADDY" UNRUH

TIL DEATH DO US PART?

Politics is one of the few professions where you can hold on to your job after you're dead. For example, Clement Woodnut Miller, a Democratic congressman from California, was killed in an airplane accident in October 1962, about a month before he would have faced the voters. Because of quirk in the state's election laws, which required a sixty-day notice prior to a special election, the well-liked Clem was allowed to keep his seat in the 88th Congress, even though he'd gone on to his reward two months before his former colleagues (who presumably each had a warm pulse) were given the oath of office. Miller's eventual successor, Donald Clausen, was elected and took office eleven days after Clem was "sworn in."

Fourteen years later, Philadelphia Democrats backed another dead man for Congress—Representative William A. Barrett, who won an April primary sixteen days after he died. The district's ward leaders then appointed a former longshoreman, Michael J. "Ozzie" Myers to run in Barrett's place in the fall election, which he won easily.

The local pols may later have wished they'd let the dead Barrett represent them: the tough-talking Myers was videotaped by FBI undercover agents accepting cash bribes in the ABSCAM sting operation. "Money talks in this business and bullshit walks. And it works the same way down in Washington," Ozzie boasted on the undercover tapes. Caught while accepting a $50,000

ABSCAM-related payoff from federal agents, Myers was taped a second time complaining he'd gotten only a $15,000 share of the bribe and wanted more!

He gained additional notoriety for his district by reportedly punching a young waitress in a suburban Virginia restaurant; evidently the congressman didn't like the service. He was honored by becoming the first House member in a hundred years to be voted out of Congress, by an overwhelming vote of 376 to 30.

That colossal misjudgment hasn't stopped municipalities in Pennsylvania from running deceased candidates, where the practice is legal, as long as the candidate is still breathing at the time of the election's filing deadline.

Congress "is the place to be if you don't love your wife, your kids are grown, and you don't like the state you come from."
—FORMER SENATOR AND 1992 DEMOCRATIC PRESIDENTIAL
CANDIDATE PAUL TSONGAS, PRESUMABLY WITH
TONGUE IN CHEEK, TO WETA PUBLIC TELEVISION
INTERVIEWER PAUL DUKE.

A LITTLE HORSE TRADING

No one believes that American elections are fixed (at least not anymore). But that doesn't mean that our modern political bosses don't occasionally make back room deals to protect a favorite incumbent or a particularly vulnerable newcomer. For example, the minutes of one Republican congressional strategy meeting reveal that top leaders from both parties had confidentially discussed the possibility of a mutual ''nonaggression'' pact in at least one state.

According to the minutes, California Rep. Tony Coelho, then chairman of the Democrats' congressional campaign committee, ''offered to withhold Democratic support from two Democratic challengers'' in the state—if the GOP would ''withhold party support" from an unidentified Republican challenger who was running against a first-term Democrat Coelho wanted to shield.

Years after resigning from Congress to become an investment banker, Coelho recalled that a Republican member from Texas had "come to me" privately in 1984 and suggested a deal in which the GOP would agree to go easy on freshman Representative Robin Tallon of South Carolina in exchange for a similar pledge from Coelho that his troops would pull their punches against Republican congressman Carroll Campbell, Jr., who later was elected governor of the state.

"I was always willing to consider protecting incumbents," Coelho admitted candidly. He added that he was "leery" about the "back channel" proposal, because a promise from the national committee didn't necessarily mean that state and local Republicans wouldn't go after his man. "I was targeting [Republican] opponents" for defeat at the time and the strategy seemed to concern his colleagues on the other side of the aisle. "I was prepared to have these discussions" and "protect" party candidates who might need extra help, Coelho said.

The former ranking Democrat concluded that he didn't recall how it all came out (Tallon was reelected), although the eyes-only minutes state that the Republican congressional campaign chief, Rep. Guy Vander Jagt of Michigan, was "strongly advised [to] avoid any arrangement with the Democrats."

STEPHEN FINDING "HIS MOTHER."

THE FINE ART OF SELF-DESTRUCTION

TOMPKINS'S TRAVAILS

The dour John Nance Garner, one of Franklin Roosevelt's vice-presidents, dismissed his office as not being worth a "pitcher of warm spit." Evidently one of Garner's predecessors in the number two spot, former New York governor Daniel Tompkins, would have agreed with that assessment. His ill-advised attempt to move from the vice-presidency back to the governor's chair led to personal and political disaster for him.

First elected vice-president on a ticket headed by James Monroe in 1816, Tompkins showed scant interest in his duties. He spent little time in Washington, and when he presided over the Senate, he seemed to wish he was somewhere else. The reason may have been that he was preoccupied by growing financial woes; the profligate Tompkins had long lived beyond his means, and creditors were hounding him.

His money troubles grew out of the War of 1812, according to writer Sol Barzman: Tompkins failed to keep adequate records for millions of dollars raised for the country's war effort. Somehow his family accounts got mixed in with official business, and he wound up $120,000 short, a sizable fortune in the early nineteenth century. What was worse, he'd become bitterly estranged from former supporter DeWitt Clinton, who succeeded Tompkins as governor of New York, and whose followers apparently helped initiate an investigation of Tompkins's debts.

No one thought that Tompkins had deliberately defrauded the government, and the New York legislature authorized the state's comptroller to give its hard-pressed former governor a special twelve percent commission on a million dollars he'd raised for the war—exactly the sum he needed to clear his shortage. All might have ended happily there, except that Tompkins held out for a *twenty-five* percent bonus, and at the same time made the grievous mistake of trying to defeat his rival Clinton for the New York governorship in 1820.

Those decisions resulted in double disaster. He lost the election to Clinton, who made certain that the New York Assembly disapproved the earlier deal to bail out Tompkins. State officials were told to sue the vice-president if necessary to get back any money he owed.

His reelection to the vice-presidency on Monroe's ticket in 1820 did nothing to halt a sudden, precipitous decline in Tompkins's behavior. He began to drink heavily, made little effort to come to Washington, and dodged creditors. Five years later he died at the age of fifty-one, a man broken and ruined by bad political judgment.

"Suppose you were an idiot. And suppose you were a member of Congress. But I repeat myself."

—MARK TWAIN

ROPE OF SAND

The presidential campaign of 1912 climaxed the bitter estrangement between two presidents who once had been close friends. The ugly, public dissolution of their relationship put Democrat Woodrow Wilson in the White House and ended an era of Republican domination of the presidency.

Theodore Roosevelt and William Howard Taft were an odd couple of American politics. Action was T.R.'s middle name, while the sedentary, 350-pound Taft was known to fall asleep after meals. The vital, high-energy Roosevelt was king of the outdoorsmen, braving a dangerous African safari well into his middle age; the Falstaffian Taft's idea of rigorous exercise was a leisurely round of golf. When circumstances didn't change fast enough to suit him, the volatile T.R. would attempt to govern by executive fiat; to the judicially minded Taft, later chief justice of the Supreme Court, the law of the land was sacrosanct, and no man or cause was above it.

Nevertheless, Roosevelt had made Taft his successor in 1908, and then watched with growing dismay as the tubby conservative failed to continue the progressive reforms T.R. had initiated. When Taft's determined standpattism resulted in a disastrous 1910 off-year election for the Republicans, the temperamental Roosevelt felt he'd been betrayed by a protégé he regarded as an incompetent heir to his reformist mantle. The former president's growing enmity for Taft became so apparent that the portly chief executive wrote sadly to a friend, "It is very hard to take all the slaps Roosevelt is handing me at this time . . . I could not subordinate my administration to him and retain my self-respect, but it is hard, very hard . . . to see a devoted friendship going to pieces like a rope of sand."

Those who thought the retiring Taft would fold his tent against the dynamic, blustery Roosevelt had another thing coming, however. He wasn't going to suffer the humiliation of being rejected as an incumbent president by his own party without a fight. "We'll hang Teddy's hat to a sour apple tree," he shouted to an enthusiastic crowd in Boston after T.R. had made plain his intention to return to power. Roosevelt partisans loved the battle and encouraged their hard-charging champion to "Hit him again, Teddy! Hit him between the eyes! Soak him! Put him over the ropes!"

Suddenly, it was difficult to imagine that the pair had ever been civil, let alone friendly. Taft became a "fathead," and a "puzzlewit" to Roosevelt, who added that his successor had "brains less than a guinea pig." Taft labeled his ex-benefactor a "demagogue" and claimed that his opponent "could not tell the truth."

When Taft used the power of the presidency to wrest the convention and the nomination from Roosevelt, who seemed to have greater popular support, T.R. characterized the outcome as "naked theft." (His delegates derisively screamed "All aboard! Choo, choo" and rubbed sandpaper together, signaling a "railroad" job, every time the convention chairman ruled against their man.)

Having earlier described himself as fit as a "bull moose," Roosevelt then deserted the convention with his wildly cheering loyalists and established the Progressive "Bull Moose" third party challenge to Taft. He proved his almost animal vigor when, after being shot by a would-be assassin, he called off a lynching crowd and proceeded to finish his campaign speech before submitting to medical treatment for a shattered rib.

In the midst of the three-way fight with Democrat Woodrow Wilson, Roosevelt sued a Michigan paper for libel for publishing a frequently repeated charge that he was an alcoholic. "I have never been drunk and never in the slightest degree under the influence of liquor," testified Roosevelt months after the election, in a trial he settled in exchange for an apology and six cents' damages.

Meanwhile, Taft had written to his wife of Roosevelt's "unscrupulousness . . . He is seeking to make his followers 'Holy Rollers,' " he complained to his spouse, who had warned that he might win the nomination, but not the election.

Mrs. Taft proved prophetic. Her husband wound up taking the worst beating to that date for an incumbent, winning only eight electoral votes. The Taft-Roosevelt feud put Wilson, a former president of Princeton University who looked the part of a schoolmaster, in the White House. The two former friends didn't speak again until a dinnertime conversation in Chicago in 1918, the final year of T.R.'s life.

"I'm not a member of any organized political party. I'm a Democrat."

—WILL ROGERS

THE HARLEM GLOBETROTTER

Kicked out of Congress and yet still electable in his own district. That was the story of Adam Clayton Powell. A handsome, charismatic black preacher from Harlem, Powell loved beautiful women, fine clothes, sun-drenched beaches, and a good time. He had no intention of taking orders from the elderly, white ruling clique that dominated Capitol Hill politics during the twenty-two years he was in office. When House Speaker Sam Rayburn gently suggested that Powell would get along better as a junior congressman if he didn't throw any of the oratorical "bombs" that had made him a legend in New York, Powell jokingly told the stocky, bald Texan that he "had a bomb in each hand" and intended to throw them immediately. He wasn't going to join the club.

While naturally gifted as a leader and speaker, Powell was also notoriously self-indulgent; his habitual junketing all over the world caused one Washington columnist to dub him "the Harlem Globetrotter." His careless approach to management caused him a seemingly endless round of legal troubles with the courts and the Internal Revenue Service over his office finances and taxes, and ultimately resulted in an arrest warrant that kept him in exile from his home state.

Eventually Powell's Lone Ranger style caught up with him, and his fellow legislators, tired of his nose-thumbing attitude, his chronic absenteeism, and allegations of nepotism, finally took action in 1966. The 89th Congress stripped Powell of his chairmanship of the powerful House Education and Labor Committee, and then by a vote of 364 to 64 refused to seat him until a special committee determined his fitness as a congressman. Harlem's hero retreated to the island of Bimini, a fishing paradise he'd made a second home.

However, when a special election was held in April 1967 for the people of the 18th District, who were without representation, their choice was the flawed but irresistible Powell, by an overwhelming margin of seven to one. "I felt as humble as any man under God could feel," Powell said. But weary of the battle, he never presented his certificate of victory to Congress and instead remained in his Caribbean retreat for several months. While his exclusion was later overturned in court, his public career was effectively all but over.

THE TWO FACES OF HENRY

For most of his adult life, Nelson Rockefeller thought it was his manifest destiny to be elected president of the United States. His last realistic shot for the Republican nomination was in 1968, and one of the biggest roadblocks in the way of fulfilling his lifelong dream was his lack of a cohesive position on the Vietnam War. Unhappily for Rocky, his toughest opponent for the top spot on the GOP ticket, Richard Nixon, was highly experienced in foreign affairs. So in 1967, the fabulously wealthy former New York governor did what came naturally; he brought in some highly paid outside experts to help figure out what to tell the voting public about Vietnam.

His top hired gun was foreign policy guru Henry Kissinger, who prepared a highly confidential "Black Book on Nixon," as a secret weapon for Rockefeller to use against his longtime rival, according to biographers Peter Collier and David Horowitz. Complete with chapter headings such as "The Tricky Dick Syndrome," and "The Loser Image," Kissinger's eyes-only analysis was a campaign primer on how to effectively undermine Nixon's attempted political comeback.

Characteristically, however, Rockefeller couldn't make up his mind what he wanted to do; his stop-and-start campaign got off late, and eventually neither he nor Ronald Reagan could block the better-organized Nixon from a first-ballot victory at the Republican convention. Kissinger, playing all the ends against the middle as usual, fawned his way into Nixon's favor and became national security advisor and later secretary of state after his patron's rival was elected president. His carefully crafted, anti-Nixon attack book was locked away in a closet and forgotten.

BRAINWASHED

One of the worst cases of political self-destruction in modern campaign history occurred in 1967, when Michigan governor George Romney literally talked himself out of contention for the 1968 Republican presidential nomination. The aborted Romney bandwagon started out on top—after his reelection in 1966, he was briefly more popular in the polls than both President Lyndon Johnson and the better-known Richard Nixon—but went downhill almost from the beginning.

Romney, like fellow GOP hopeful Nelson Rockefeller, just couldn't seem to come up with a coherent policy on Vietnam, the most important issue for anyone wishing to move into the White House in 1968. Every time he opened his mouth on the campaign trail, confusion grew over exactly what the governor, not exactly a spellbinding speaker, meant. Finally, in August 1967, he truly, although unintentionally, put his foot into it.

On a Detroit television program, Romney tried to clarify his inconsistent previous statements by saying, "Well, you know, when I came back from Vietnam, I just had the greatest brainwashing that anybody can get . . . Not only by the generals, but also by the diplomatic corps over there, and they do a very thorough job . . . And, as a result, I've changed my mind . . . I no longer believe that it was necessary for us to get involved in South Vietnam to stop Communist aggression."

What candidate Romney was trying to say, in his own convoluted fashion, was that he'd reexamined his views in the two years since he'd visited Vietnam and now opposed the Johnson administration's policy of intervention. That didn't matter, however, in the howl of protest and derision that followed the off-the-cuff "brainwashing" remark. Editorialists noted that Romney had previously supported LBJ, and that his crack about being brainwashed made him sound like a politician who was easily influenced. One careless descriptive phrase shattered his credibility.

Almost overnight, Romney's standing plummeted, and for all practical purposes, he was through as a serious contender.

ORIGIN OF THE ENEMIES' LIST

Perhaps Richard Nixon's worst character flaw was his career-long obsession with a variety of perceived enemies, many unseen, whom he believed were out to get him. His gut-level instinct to either strike first, or hit back harder when criticized, invariably

produced his most embarrassing moments. By the time he reached the White House, after more than twenty years in national politics, he'd surrounded himself with younger subordinates and "yes men" who fed this insecurity and helped turn it into a paranoia that bordered on the obsessive.

Proof that the Nixon White House was careening off in a dangerous and self-destructive direction was found in an August 16, 1971, memo by Nixon's counsel, John Dean, entitled "Dealing With Our Political Enemies." Dean audaciously suggested that White House staff members collect names of Nixon opponents "whom we should be giving a hard time."

"The project coordinator" of Dean's nasty little hit team would then "determine what sorts of dealings these individuals have with the Federal Government and how we can best screw them" by withholding federal contracts, initiating prosecutions, and cutting off their taxpayer grants.

This little seven-paragraph outline was the genesis of the much more ambitious Nixon "enemies' list," which was later assembled by Nixon hatchet man Charles Colson and contained the names of scores of political opponents, celebrities, media figures, labor leaders, academics, and businessmen.

Included were ten Democratic senators, all twelve black representatives, contributors to potential future Nixon election opponents, and a Philadelphia security firm that, as a "heavy [Hubert] Humphrey contributor . . . could program his agency against us." Even the New York Jets' star football quarterback, Joe Namath, not exactly a political heavyweight, was among those listed to be watched for further signs of anti-Nixon tendencies.

BLUNDER-BUTZ

Years worth of glacier-like progress by the Republican party to attract more black voters was handed an embarrassing setback because of an offhand, off-color joke repeated by President Gerald Ford's agriculture secretary, Earl Butz, during the 1976 presidential campaign.

Days after the GOP convention, the wise-cracking Butz was hobnobbing with show business celebrities Pat Boone and Sonny Bono on a plane flight to Mexico. Clean-cut singer Boone, a long-time Republican enthusiast, innocently asked the cabinet officer why so few black voters supported the Ford-Dole ticket.

"The only things that coloreds are looking for in life are tight pussy, loose shoes and a warm place to shit," Butz replied, thinking his locker room response would go no further. Unfortunately, however, another participant in the conversation was John Dean, President Nixon's former White House counsel. After confessing his administration's Watergate crimes to Congress and federal grand juries, Dean had become, ironically, a reporter—covering the Republican convention for the counter-culture magazine *Rolling Stone*. Just a few years before, the left-leaning publication had been high on his former colleagues' hate list.

Without naming Butz as the source, Dean repeated the racist line in his subsequent story, attributing it to a member of the Ford cabinet. It didn't take other campaign journalists long to discover the identity of the guilty party, and Butz was forced to resign amidst the front-page political fallout that followed the disclosure of his crude remark. Party strategists, needless to say, had a hard time explaining Butz's thoughtless blunder to minority voters being courted by the Republicans.

GEMSTONE

Perhaps the most patently illegal of the Nixon reelection campaign's dirty-tricks plots, "Gemstone" was a scaled-down version of an even more farfetched espionage operation originally devised by the Committee to Re-Elect The President (CREEP) henchman Gordon Liddy. Gemstone involved actual break-ins and safecrackings aimed at stealing information from perceived Nixon enemies; it included a secret, June 1972 attempt to burglarize the office of the Democratic national committee at the Watergate, an ultimately bungled effort that triggered the downfall of the Nixon White House.

While Attorney General John Mitchell had rejected an earlier Liddy-devised spying scenario, which included utilizing a yacht and ship-bound prostitutes to compromise Democrats at their 1972 national convention, he looked more favorably upon an only slightly less outrageous scheme to break into the Las Vegas safe of publisher Hank Greenspun. Nixon had long been annoyed by press reports alleging that his ne'er-do-well brother Donald had received a $200,000 loan from billionaire financier Howard Hughes in return for some unspecified favors. When it was revealed that crusading editor Greenspun, a man of many connections, had hundreds of Hughes's documents in his possession, Mitchell authorized a black bag job in Greenspun's office to find out if he had any proof of Nixon malfeasance. A second target approved by Mitchell was the Watergate complex housing the Washington office of the Democratic national committee chairman, Larry O'Brien, a longtime Nixon nemesis.

When the Watergate burglars were later caught in the act, Nixon's minions ensured their president's downfall by covering up their clumsy, ill-advised actions. White House counsel John Dean ordered the Secret Service to steal Gemstone-related documents from the safe of Watergate conspirator Howard Hunt, and then turned the papers over to the FBI for destruction. Meanwhile, Nixon campaign deputy Jeb Stuart Magruder burned the rest of the Gemstone file, claiming he was acting on direct orders from Mitchell.

President Nixon rejected suggestions that he make his friend Mitchell the scapegoat for the Watergate fiasco, but he did replace him at CREEP with former Minnesota congressman Clark MacGregor. "We'll clean the son of a bitch up," Nixon vowed, referring to the Keystone Kops antics of his CREEP reelection committee, "and we'll run this campaign."

Almost two years later, when the roof caved in on him, Nixon still didn't blame his pipe-puffing attorney general for bringing him down. The fault, he was convinced, lay with Mitchell's boozy, outspoken wife Martha, who had driven her husband to distraction with her demands that he leave politics, and her unwelcome public pronouncements on the Watergate follies. As

Nixon biographer Stephen Ambrose noted, the fallen chief executive thought a woman was to blame for the ultimate ruination of his White House. "Without Martha," Nixon wrote in his diary, "I am sure this Watergate thing would never have happened."

THE WOMAN I LOVE

Not many newlyweds spend their honeymoon campaigning. But when they married in August 1974, Maryland governor Marvin Mandel and his second wife, Jeanne Dorsey, weren't just any couple. Short, balding, middle-aged Marvin Mandel hadn't been regarded as a political lothario. Nevertheless, his surprising public pronouncement the summer before that he was leaving his wife Barbara "Bootsie" Mandel, to wed a much younger divorcée with several children, was a publicity bombshell that ignited a bizarre, preelection marital standoff. Mandel was officially divorced from his wife of thirty-two years for only thirty minutes before marrying the blond, beautiful Jeanne.

Although the governor had privately told Bootsie that he was in love with the striking Mrs. Dorsey and wanted a divorce, he was unprepared for her rather unusual reaction. Bootsie simply pretended her husband had taken leave of his senses and refused to vacate the governor's mansion in Annapolis for six months. She barricaded herself in the fifty-four-room, 104-year-old Georgian mansion and, like Dickens's Mrs. Haversham, acted as though nothing had changed. The embarrassed and suddenly homeless chief executive assumed residence, first in a hotel and then an apartment, waiting a year for his divorce to become finalized. Bootsie finally gave up the Alamo in Annapolis and moved out, much to the governor's relief.

Even after Mandel married Jeanne, however, the opinionated Bootsie kept firing back at the new First Couple. "No one bothered to let me know that I was even divorced, let alone that he remarried. The governor would have shown better taste if he had waited a while.

"Why, she was living in the mansion with him after I left.

There she was committing adultery in front of her children . . .
Now, I ask you—How can you be a First Lady if you're not a
lady first?'' commented the former Mrs. Mandel bluntly, not
exactly boosting her ex-husband's reelection bid.

If the tale of Mandel's mansion contained enough embarrassment for a political lifetime, the governor's reelection campaign
was the beginning of a downward spiral for him. Despite the
humiliating soap opera scene in the capital, Mandel won reelection; but his personal finances soon attracted the attention of
federal prosecutors, and several of his closest associates were
indicted on various criminal charges. What one writer called the
"tawdry aroma of machine politics" smoldered in the ashes of
the unexpected marital war. Mandel was later indicted, found
guilty, and jailed on mail fraud and other charges. Years and
many appeals later, however, his conviction was overturned by
an appeals court and he returned to public life, with the hard-won
Jeanne still at his side.

THE TEFLON LEGISLATOR

Michigan congressman Donald W. Riegle faced what should have
been an uphill battle when he ran for the U.S. Senate in 1976.
Once a loyal Republican, he'd switched over to the Democrats
just four years before. He'd hardly warmed his seat in Congress
when, while still in his twenties, he boasted openly about running
for president. In addition, his older, more experienced colleagues
in the House hadn't appreciated the young upstart's 1972 book,
"*O Congress,*" in which he'd lectured his elders about the bun-
gling mess he thought they were making of the nation's business.

All Riegle's baggage, however, was just a mild prelude to the
firestorm of controversy that erupted just before the Senate election, when it was disclosed in the *Detroit News* that the married
congressman, who had three children, had engaged in a torrid
affair in 1969 with a comely, unpaid staff volunteer, and that
she'd tape-recorded their amorous conversations.

Incredibly, Riegle knew that his twenty-one-year-old lover was taping their intimate talks, during which she called herself by the code name "Dorothy," and referred to him as "Prince." Far from keeping his extramarital, bedroom adventures to himself, Riegle freely told his staff members about assignations with Dorothy. On one of the tapes, for example, Prince said to Dorothy that he'd told one of his female employees "what an exquisite session we had . . . I think she was flabbergasted."

Laughing, Dorothy replied, "She didn't think I had it in me."

"Oh, God. No, no. She knew you had it in you, all right," Riegle told his paramour. Later it was disclosed that Riegle had called his Dorothy from all over the country, including George Bush's Houston bedroom, and from a lobby in Louisville, where he was attending the Kentucky Derby.

When news of the tapes broke, Riegle called published reports of the affair "another example of mudslinging journalism." His political position didn't improve when it was revealed that he'd dumped Dorothy after several months and divorced his wife to marry another woman in his congressional office, one who'd been regaled with stories about his sexual escapades with Dorothy.

Apparently Michigan voters didn't mind the juicy tidbits concerning the congressman's between-the-sheets antics—he won election to the Senate. In 1991, an older Don Riegle, by then chairman of the powerful Senate Banking Committee, came under intense scrutiny from the Senate Ethics Committee for his heavily criticized role in the savings and loan scandal.

NO KIDDING, TED

"We're facing complex issues and problems in this nation at this time, but we have faced similar challenges at other times. And the energies and the resourcefulness of this nation, I think, should be focused on these problems in a way that brings a sense of restoration in this country by its people to—in dealing with the problems that we

face—primarily the problems of energy. And I would basically feel that—that it's imperative for this country to either move forward, that it can't stand still, or otherwise it moves back."
—Senator Edward Kennedy to CBS interviewer Roger Mudd, on why he was running for president in 1980. This response effectively ended his election year primary challenge to Jimmy Carter.

PATRONAGE PROBLEMS

One of the prime perks of being elected to Congress is the availability of hundreds of political patronage jobs, such as the largely unnecessary job of operating the Capitol's numerous elevators. These sinecures are doled out to faithful supporters and children of generous campaign contributors. The lucky holders of these coveted positions are expected to know their place on the congressional plantation, and to treat their elected benefactors like privileged lords of the manor.

Occasionally, though, this master-serf relationship can backfire, as it did in 1982–83, when at least ten employees from the House Doorkeepers office were arrested during a drug-selling investigation. Shudders of anxiety swept through the corridors of the Capitol buildings when it was learned that several of the young suspects claimed to have delivered cocaine and marijuana to members' offices.

The House Ethics Committee hired superlawyer Joe Califano to conduct a separate probe at a cost of $1.5 million. The fallout from his detailed report and the separate federal criminal investigations helped derail several once-promising political careers.

There was "substantial evidence" that three former congressmen had used cocaine and other drugs while in office. Rep. Barry Goldwater, Jr., of California had given up his House seat in 1982 in an unsuccessful run for the Senate. He denied "uncategorically" that he'd used drugs, but Justice Department officials had secretly taped conversations of him discussing drugs with a woman involved with the narcotics ring. The publicity damaged Goldwater's further political aspirations.

Former Rep. John Burton of California, known for erratic behavior in Congress, told reporters when his name surfaced that he hadn't used drugs. Later, he admitted to ABC-TV that he'd spent $100,000 on cocaine over six years while in Congress and that it had turned his life "upside down."

Ex-Rep. Fred Richmond of New York had already served time in prison for income tax evasion and marijuana possession by the time the Califano report was published. Jail apparently was the only way to keep the popular but troubled Richmond out of office, as he had been reelected twice since 1978 after admitting he'd illegally solicited an undercover Washington policeman for sex.

While Califano downplayed the magnitude of the drug sales, other members' names surfaced during the probe and the scandal became an election issue in several districts.

"I am the only certified 'not guilty' candidate of either party."

—FORMER TEXAS GOVERNOR AND PRESIDENTIAL CANDIDATE JOHN CONNALLY, CITING HIS ACQUITTAL ON BRIBERY CHARGES. (CONNALLY, WHO ONCE SERVED AS TREASURY SECRETARY, SPENT A REPORTED $12 MILLION ON A 1980 CAMPAIGN THAT NETTED EXACTLY ONE REPUBLICAN PARTY DELEGATE.)

GEORGIA DAWGFIGHT

The University of Georgia Bulldogs aren't the only hard hitters in the Atlanta area. That was proven in 1984, when clean-cut Republican candidate Pat Swindall, running on a Christian morality

Another voice for Cleveland.

platform, pulled off something that rarely happens—he beat an entrenched congressional incumbent, Elliott Levitas, with some rather unusual tactics.

Part of the Swindall campaign was effective boilerplate strategy; he utilized the immense popularity of his party's White House ticket, featuring Ronald Reagan, and linked his opponent to the Democrats' vice-presidential candidate, Geraldine Ferraro, who apparently wasn't too popular in that particular southern district.

Other Swindall techniques, as described by political advertising writer Montague Kerns, were more imaginative. He charged that Levitas had traded his vote on a bill in order to get the administration's under secretary of the Treasury to cancel a personal appearance at a Swindall fund-raiser. Then he called the official and taped the conversation, whose response seemed to confirm his allegation that Levitas was engaged in "power brokering" in Washington. Swindall also successfully turned the tables on his foe and accused Levitas of a "Goebbels-like" attack on Swindall's failure to make timely payments of his income taxes.

The ousted Levitas, who believed Ronald Reagan's landslide victory was the key to his own defeat, had the last laugh, however. Four years later Swindall lost his hard-won seat amid exposure of his negotiations for a home loan funded with money from illegal drug and gambling activities. Unfortunately for the young congressman, his embarrassing-sounding comments concerning the controversial source of the loan money were recorded on tape.

MONKEY BUSINESS

"He's always in jeopardy of having the sex issue raised if he can't keep his pants on," was how one frustrated aide explained the perplexing enigma named Gary Hart. The former Colorado senator, George McGovern's campaign manager while still in his early thirties, made a strong run at the 1984 Democratic presidential nomination, until Walter Mondale effectively challenged

Hart's "campaign of ideas" by asking dryly, "Where's the beef?"

Many observers thought that the bushy-haired, cerebral Hart was on his way to personal and political disaster well before he entered the 1988 campaign for another run at the presidency. The shortening of his name from "Hartpence," and poorly explained discrepancies concerning his true age left some voters wondering about Hart's judgment and credibility. Somewhat incongruously for a professional politician, movie star Warren Beatty became his closest confidant, and Hart seemed fascinated with the free and easy Hollywood life-style of the actor, with nubile young starlets roaming in and out of Beatty's Los Angeles household.

Not only Hart's aides, but journalists covering the candidate knew about his years of habitual womanizing. Yet they were reluctant to reveal it because Hart's wife Lee, although estranged from her husband for a good part of their twenty-five-year marriage, had loyally agreed to hit the presidential campaign trail with her sometime spouse. Confident that no one would call his bluff, Hart arrogantly threw down the gauntlet to the press and dared them to produce evidence that he was anything other than a faithful family man.

"Follow me around, I don't care. I'm serious. If anyone wants to put a tail on me, go ahead. They'd be very bored," he told the *New York Times Magazine.* Unfortunately for Hart, the *Miami Herald* did just that, assigning reporters to shadow the glamorous candidate who was hiding a secret life. It wasn't long before the stealthy scribes discovered their quarry at a Washington town house with a young, shapely blond named Donna Rice, a some-time model whose real avocation was professional party girl.

Hart swore there hadn't been any hanky-panky behind closed doors, but within days *The National Enquirer* tabloid published a photo that was fatal to his candidacy; he was pictured sitting on the boat *Monkey Business* in Bimini, smiling with drink in hand and the tousle-haired Rice sitting undemurely in his lap. It was all over, and everyone but Hart and a few stubborn hangers-on seemed to know it; he became the butt of television's late night comedians, a sure sign of doom.

When reporters from the *Washington Post* told Hart they had evidence of another, previous extramarital affair, Hart asked his press secretary wearily, "This is never going to end, is it?" Reluctantly, he dropped out of the campaign and retreated to a Colorado estate he'd bought with money loaned to him by his pal Beatty.

Apparently not yet through flagellating himself, however, Hart inexplicably returned to the campaign wars, although his support had dwindled to a negligible level. After being treated as a campaign oddity for months, he quit a second time. Donna Rice modeled the "No Excuses" line of jeans before fading back into obscurity.

WHAT'S ITALIAN FOR *CHUTZPAH?*

"I have an absolutely unblemished record . . . I am absolutely incorruptible."
—REP. MARIO BIAGGI (D-NY), FOLLOWING FELONY CONVICTIONS FOR ACCEPTING ILLEGAL GRATUITIES AND OBSTRUCTION OF JUSTICE. AFTER THAT CURIOUS STATEMENT, BIAGGI WAS CONVICTED IN A SECOND CRIMINAL TRIAL ON SEPARATE FELONY CHARGES RELATING TO THE WEDTECH INFLUENCE-PEDDLING SCANDAL, RESIGNED HIS SEAT, DESPITE THE FACT HE PROBABLY COULD HAVE BEEN REELECTED, AND SERVED TWENTY-SIX MONTHS IN FEDERAL PRISON.

SASSO'S SWAN SONG

Presidential campaigns are sometimes like stumbling basketball teams—too often, even when there's plenty of talent and hustle, they just don't have the right chemistry. Opportunities for what should be easy shots end up instead being clumsily thrown out of bounds. That unfortunate tendency was evident in Michael

Dukakis's snakebitten campaign even before the Democrats chose him as their standard-bearer in 1988. What should have been a hard-but-clean campaign tactic turned instead into an unmitigated disaster in September 1987. As a result, the Dukakis team was stripped of the man who, aside from the candidate himself, might have been their most valuable player.

John Sasso, Dukakis's first campaign manager, in the words of the candidate himself, was "like a brother"; one of the few people who had the cerebral Massachusetts governor's trust. Having always wanted to run a presidential campaign, Sasso was determined that no other Democrat derail his dream of going all the way to the White House over George Bush's prone body. One potential roadblock was the attractive, articulate senator from Delaware, Joe Biden, who possessed a golden, if overused, tongue and an uncanny ability to raise big bucks—two critical attributes for a presidential hopeful. Sasso schemed to get Biden off the campaign trail and back in Washington, his tail between his legs.

Biden's Achilles' heel was that he liked to hear himself talk— and talk—"bloviate," as another world-class political gabber, Warren Harding, called it. When he got carried away at the Iowa state fair and lifted not only the words, but the emotional gestures and delivery, of a speech by British Labor party leader Neil Kinnock without attribution, Sasso got an inspiration. First he tipped reporters that Biden had plagiarized—then to prove it, he had a campaign intern splice together a videotape of the speech for limited distribution as indisputable evidence. Don't finger the Dukakis camp as the accusers, was the only condition he and his cohort Paul Tully placed on interested reporters.

As quickly as a summer storm, Biden's bubble burst. Media coverage of his past actions intensified dramatically; almost immediately, he was accused of cribbing words on a paper in law school, and using Kinnock's phrases without giving credit at another political function. When he was taped losing his temper and misrepresenting his academic record in New Hampshire, the loquacious senator's presidential hopes for 1988 perished.

Pointing out possible plagiarism on the part of a rival candidate isn't necessarily a nefarious act in itself, and compared to what went on later in the general election, Sasso's backstage shot at Biden was tame. But then he compounded a minor sin by failing to fully inform Dukakis about his role in Biden's demise. When the little "Duke" uprightly suggested that he'd probably fire anyone who'd leaked such a damaging story, he sealed Sasso's doom. Worse yet for Dukakis, when the identity of Biden's tormentors became publicly known, he was torn between two warring factions of advisers—half told him to dump Sasso and the other half insisted that he back up his beleaguered manager.

He chose the worst alternative—he vacillated. His wishywashy decision to suspend Sasso from the campaign for two weeks satisfied no one, and in fact, disgusted several prominent Democratic supporters, who defected to other candidates. Sasso voluntarily resigned to relieve Dukakis of his terminal indecisiveness, but the loss of the savvy campaign manager left the candidate deeply wounded and saddened. Even after Sasso was replaced, many Dukakis loyalists waited like expectant children for his return to a campaign that was never again quite the same. When the prodigal son did finally return to the fold, it was too late.

HYMIETOWN

Jesse Jackson, one of the most gifted practitioners of media manipulation in the modern era, almost had his 1984 presidential campaign derailed by a tasteless, offhand remark he made in front of several reporters. It was the same kind of thoughtless, racial crack that Jackson previously had castigated other public figures for uttering.

Amidst the artificial heat generated by the wintry February electioneering, the *Washington Post* turned up the temperature yet another few degrees when it reported, in a story about Jackson's difficult relationship with the Jewish community, that the black activist had referred to Jews as "Hymies" and to New York City as "Hymietown." Oddly, perhaps since the remark was buried in the account, and because Jackson had thought the session was off-the-record, there was little attention paid to the slur for almost a week. However, the source of the quote was respected black editor Milton Coleman of the *Post's* national staff, who had personally overheard Jackson using the terms in what Jackson thought was a harmless bull session with reporters.

Then after a poor showing in the Iowa caucus, Jackson suddenly was besieged with questions about the statement. More than two weeks after the *Post* story, Jackson insistently told CBS News that "It is simply not true," and he boldly insisted that his accuser come forward with evidence. Almost a week and scores of inquiries later, though, the candidate backed off from his persistent denial and termed the remark "innocent and unintended."

Unused to what he called an unfriendly "hounding" by a usually worshipful press, Jackson also came under fire from angry Jewish voters, many of whom already were suspicious of his views about the Jewish faith and the State of Israel, in particular. Irate, Jackson at one point almost hysterically threatened to sue the *Post* for libel, but after the paper reaffirmed he'd made the statements in question, the preacher-politician backed off and backpedaled on his absolute denials. At that point, few believed them anyway.

"Hymiegate" didn't ruin the Jackson campaign, but it temporarily tainted the media-savvy Jackson's credibility with the voters and the press alike.

SENATOR, YOU'RE NO JACK KENNEDY

When Senator Lloyd Bentsen told Dan Quayle that he was "no Jack Kennedy" during the 1988 vice-presidential debate, he may have been closer to the mark than even he realized. Seven years earlier, while Quayle was serving as an Indiana congressman, he was caught up in a sex scandal involving a shapely blond lobbyist named Paula Parkinson; the incident came back to haunt him briefly during the 1988 presidential campaign.

Paula's third husband, an affable lobbyist named Hank Parkinson, said his wife, who once posed provocatively for *Playboy*

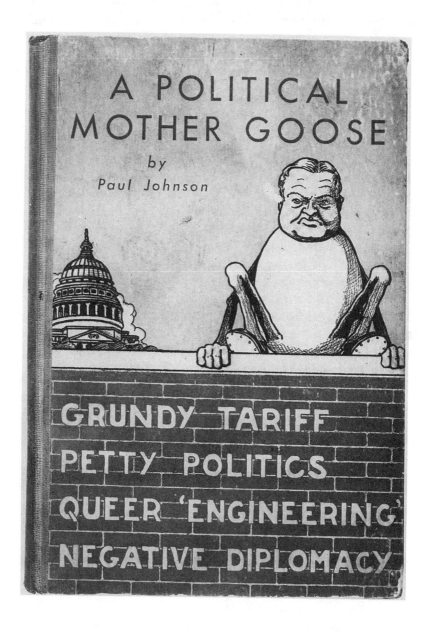

magazine, could make " 'Please pass the butter,' sound like an exciting proposition.'' Evidently a lot of men agreed with that assessment. Among her other self-confessed bedroom adventures, the well-endowed Mrs. Parkinson reportedly had an extramarital fling with Quayle's Republican House colleague, Tom Evans of Delaware.

During a Florida golf outing in January 1980, Quayle made the unfortunate decision to share a cottage—paid for by a tobacco lobbyist—with Evans, Paula, and Illinois congressman Tom Railsback. When *Wilmington News-Journal* reporter Joe Trento learned of the cozy arrangement and wrote a front-page story about it, several Washington politicians who'd enjoyed dalliances with Paula scrambled for cover. Quayle and Railsback insisted they'd had nothing to do with either Paula or the sleeping arrangements. "I didn't have one single thing to do with that woman," Railsback claimed. "Do you think I'd be in that damn house if I knew that damn blond bombshell would be down there?"

Although Paula's lobbying skills were limited to her considerable sensual appeal, an FBI investigation was undertaken to determine whether there'd been any sex-for-votes hanky-panky between Mrs. Parkinson and her political paramours. But the well-publicized probe ended with an inconclusive whimper, and soon pretty Paula faded into obscurity in Mesquite, Texas, after ruining the reputation of Evans. Previous to the titillating Parkinson episode, the Delaware congressman had been considered for a cabinet post in the Reagan administration, but afterward fell out of favor at the White House and wound up being defeated for reelection in 1982.

Then in 1988, George Bush shocked his supporters and Republican stalwarts by selecting the little-known junior senator from Indiana as his running mate. During the campaign, *Penthouse* published assertions that the boyish-looking Quayle had sexually propositioned the comely Paula during the infamous golf outing in 1980, but that she'd supposedly spurned his advances.

"He was putting the moves on me," Paula told a *Penthouse* interviewer. One of Paula's former attorneys claimed that she'd reported Quayle's advances to the FBI in 1981. Quayle denied that he'd sought her favors, and the accusation blew over without substantial political damage.

Given his well-chronicled sexual conquests, it's unlikely that Jack Kennedy would have passed up such a tempting amorous opportunity, however; so Bentsen's campaign debate assertion was absolutely accurate. Dan Quayle is no JFK!

THE CLAYTIE AND ANN SHOW

"It's been a disgusting campaign," complained one turned-off voter, describing the 1990 Texas gubernatorial race between Republican Clayton Williams and Democrat Ann Richards. "Do you have a place where I can push 'None Of The Above'?" asked another irritated Lone Star resident.

Their dismay was well founded. Until this no-holds-barred contest, the biggest waste of campaign money in Texas had been former Governor "Big Jawn" Connally's expenditure of more than $11 million to secure exactly one delegate in the 1980 presidential sweepstakes (Mrs. Ada Mills of Clarksville, Arkansas, worried afterward that she'd be forever known as "the $11 million delegate").

The blundering Williams, a millionaire rancher, spent a reported $20 million to put on a campaign that could charitably be characterized as an unmitigated disaster. "Claytie" just didn't know when to keep his mouth shut. On one occasion, he had to apologize to voters for an inexplicable remark in which he compared rape to bad weather. Then Williams proceeded to prove to voters that he hadn't even a basic grasp of the political issues in the campaign by fumbling a simple question over how he had voted on a constitutional amendment on the state ballot. " . . . All I can say is I just forgot. I forgot, Boy Scout honor."

Some of his supporters poked fun at Richards, a recovering alcoholic, and suggested that perhaps she hadn't stopped hitting the bottle, or that she should take a drug test. Williams also refused to debate Richards, a former state treasurer, because she refused to sign what he termed a "no negative campaign pledge."

No shrinking violet herself, the grandmotherly looking Richards slung her fair share of the mud as well. She publicly questioned Williams's relationship with a Houston loan broker, and Richards's backers broadly hinted about shady details in Williams's financial affairs, rumors that the wealthy rancher regarded as untrue and slanderous.

It's difficult to single out the lowest moment among the many in this campaign, but it was probably during their joint appearance in the crowded campaign ballroom in Dallas. Furious at Richards's accusations about his financial dealings and other cutting remarks, Williams decided to confront his opponent. When she offered her hand to shake, Williams refused, saying "I'm here to call you a liar today."

"I'm sorry, Clayton," Richards said.

"That's what you are," Claytie replied testily.

While candidates in Texas had refused to shake hands before, many voters apparently thought the gesture ungentlemanly and ungallant when directed at a lady candidate. The public exchange, yet another chapter in what the *San Antonio News Express* called "Gabby Hayes Meets Calamity Jane" also gave the Richards campaign an opportunity to produce a life-sized poster of her offering her hand—for five dollars, voters could pose with it for a picture.

Richards emerged from the muck and was elected, largely because Williams self-destructed with his series of bone-headed pronouncements.

"TAI" AS IN "SAY"

For sheer, self-destructive perversity, it's tough to top the decade-long political power struggle between Virginia's straight-arrow Democratic senator, lantern-jawed, ex-marine Chuck Robb, and the Old Dominion's white-haired, slightly paranoid governor, Douglas Wilder. The all-too-public feud has been similar to the four-round, multiple-knockdown, brutal heavyweight fight between George Foreman and Ron Lyle; each just kept slugging in the middle of the ring, crashing to the canvas and getting up, until only one was left standing (in that instance, Foreman). But at the end, neither contender was ever quite the same again.

The nasty slugfest, which each has unsuccessfully tried to conceal, would be pathetic if it wasn't so entertaining. The mutual backstabbing had all the elements of a major political scandal: sex, spying, threats, lying, fired aides, and a criminal investigation. The electoral odd couple, whose political careers are "intertwined like Southern wisteria," according to one Virginia columnist, began their battle royale in earnest in 1982. Robb, a son-in-law of former president Lyndon Johnson and at the time Virginia's governor, offered a Democratic candidate for the U.S. Senate who was unacceptably conservative to Wilder; he impolitely threatened to bolt from the state's Democratic party and run on his own. When the dust cleared, Wilder had won the initial power struggle and Robb was left red-faced.

Three years later, after Robb had helped an all-Democratic ticket sweep into the state's three top elective offices, he was attacked by a Wilder aide for taking too much of the credit for the victory. Enraged, the normally introverted Robb released two strongly worded letters he'd sent to Wilder, relating his "extreme unhappiness" and threatening to withhold his support for lieutenant governor Wilder's future bid for the governorship. Another missive bluntly accused Wilder of "deliberate distortions and untruths, and the blindsiding of allies without at least trying to resolve differences first." Wilder ignored Robb's complaints. Meanwhile, rumors circulated that Robb, everybody's boy scout while governor, had been present at parties during which cocaine was used.

The ill will hung ominously in the air until Wilder was elected governor by a razor-thin margin in 1989, and it became clear that both men harbored ambitions to inhabit the White House. Then the real fun began. First Robb filed a formal complaint with the Federal Election Commission, alleging that state Republican leaders illegally had raised funds from GOP activists to pay the expenses of a private detective, Billy Franklin, who had pursued the drug allegations against Robb like a bloodhound.

Things really got ugly in April 1991, when an NBC News program, "Exposé," broadcast the charges of a shapely former

beauty queen, Tai Collins, that she'd had an eighteen-month affair with Senator Robb while he was governor, and that Robb aides repeatedly threatened her with retribution if she went public with the details of her trysts with the married Robb. "If it takes me twenty years, I'm going to do everything I possibly can to see that [detective Franklin] pays an extraordinarily high price," said one of Robb's top aides in a secretly taped conversation with Tai aired on the NBC broadcast.

"I lost my innocence in this ordeal," she lamented, although she got over her embarrassment long enough to pose in the buff for *Playboy* magazine. The senator denied having sex with the lithe platinum blond, but conceded that he'd shared a bottle of wine with her in a hotel room, where she'd provided a relaxing, but nonsexual massage.

Wilder ordered the Virginia state police to conduct a formal probe into whether the senator's aides had pressured the stunning Ms. Collins into maintaining her silence. Infuriated, Robb claimed that Wilder used the investigation to discredit him. Then the dispute *really* began to degenerate.

Weeks later, it was revealed that for more than two years, Robb's aides had in their possession at least one tape recording of Wilder discussing his rivalry with Robb from a cellular telephone and concluding that Robb was "finished" politically because of the bad publicity concerning his personal life. "It's wiretapping and it's a criminal act," Wilder responded, when the covert taping was disclosed. The furor resulted in a federal grand jury investigation, during which Robb testified; meanwhile, he was forced to jettison three of his top aides who were accused of involvement in acquiring and concealing the controversial tapes.

Wilder couldn't seem to leave well enough alone, though, and pushed his longstanding grudge, weirdly insisting that there was an eavesdropping device on a tree outside his office, an assertion that was quickly discounted by overworked police investigators. Later, when Wilder decided to throw his hat into the ring to unsuccessfully seek the Democratic presidential nomination, he attracted additional skeptical attention when his young female press secretary, Laura Dillard, was forced out for being critical of the governor's lack of attention to state business. Robb, according to media accounts, pulled himself into a turtle shell, refusing to accept the extent of the damage to his once-vaunted reputation as "Mr. Clean."

The Virginia soap opera didn't help Senate Democrats, whose fund-raising activities were being supervised by the beleaguered Robb.

I'M ONE OF THE DEADBEATS?

Sometimes in elective politics, it just comes back and hits you right in the face. Ask Larry Hopkins, a well-regarded Kentucky Republican who minded his own business, and that of his bluegrass constituents, for thirteen years in Congress. Then, unfortunately, he decided he wanted to be governor of his home state. By most accounts a decent, friendly politician, Hopkins battled his way through a difficult primary to take on a better-financed Democratic lieutenant governor with the very Southern name of Brereton Jones, who had a huge advantage in party voter registration in his favor.

In today's campaigns, when you're way down, it's time to get tough. Larry did just that, bringing in the nasty boys from the GOP advertising world and going after Mr. Jones's financial background, which didn't look that rosy. One ad pictured Hopkins's opponent with a "For Sale" sign hung around his neck, and other spots suggested that Jones had to win the election in order to resolve supposedly serious debt problems caused by his horse-breeding business.

The in-your-face strategy worked initially, according to an account in the *Washington Post,* and Hopkins began to creep up in the polls. However, then a nationwide story broke concerning the congressional check-bouncing scandal. Dozens of careless legislators were getting special treatment from the House bank, which covered their rubber checks at no cost. Taxpayers, who pay as much as twenty-five dollars or more when their personal checks aren't covered at the local bank, understandably weren't

thrilled about the revelations that they were underwriting a check kiting system on Capitol Hill.

Since the bank was controlled by the Democrats, a number conservative GOP lawmakers, such as Hopkins's fellow Republican Harold Rogers, went home to their districts and blasted t malefactors. The overdrawn congressmen, wrote Rogers in blistering missive to his constituents, should be "fired." Sadl Rogers apparently didn't realize (or didn't care) that his cc league Hopkins had overdrawn thirty-two checks, totaling mc than $4,000, during the previous year.

Not surprisingly, the backlash concerning his sloppy chec book balancing quickly finished any chance that Hopkins had pulling off an upset, and he was soundly defeated.

thrilled about the revelations that they were underwriting a check-kiting system on Capitol Hill.

Since the bank was controlled by the Democrats, a number of conservative GOP lawmakers, such as Hopkins's fellow Republican Harold Rogers, went home to their districts and blasted the malefactors. The overdrawn congressmen, wrote Rogers in a blistering missive to his constituents, should be "fired." Sadly, Rogers apparently didn't realize (or didn't care) that his colleague Hopkins had overdrawn thirty-two checks, totaling more than $4,000, during the previous year.

Not surprisingly, the backlash concerning his sloppy checkbook balancing quickly finished any chance that Hopkins had of pulling off an upset, and he was soundly defeated.

READ!!

PAUSE and REFLECT.

Van Buren in favor of Negroes voting, and opposed to the Poor White Man's enjoying this inestimable privilege!

Extracts from the "Reports of the proceedings and "debates of the convention of 1821, assembled "for the purpose of amending the constitution of "the State of New-York." These Reports were taken at the time and published in 1821.

It appears from page 178 of this volume, that on the 19th of September, 1821, the convention proceeded to consider the subject of the Elective Franchise, and that the Report upon that subject, made by Mr. Sandford, was taken up. This report proposed, as a part of the constitution, that "every "*white* male citizen of 21 years who shall have "been one year an inhabitant of this State, and for "six months a resident in the town, county or dis-"trict where he may offer his vote, &c. &c., shall "be entitled to vote, &c."

In submitting this report, Mr. Sandford addressed the convention at length—and was followed by Mr. Ross, who, in the course of his argument, in favor of the Report, used the following language:

"That all men are free and equal, according to the usual declarations, applies to them only in a state of nature, and not after the institution of civil government; for then many rights, flowing from a natural equality, are necessarily abridged, with a view to produce the greatest amount of security and happiness to the whole community. On this principle the right of suffrage is extended to white men only. But why, it will probably be asked, are blacks to be excluded? I answer, because they are seldom, if ever, required to share in the common burthens or defence of the State. There are also additional reasons; they are a peculiar people, incapable, in my judgment, of exercising that privilege with any sort of discretion, prudence, or Independence. They have no just conceptions of civil liberty. They know not how to appreciate it, and are consequently indifferent to its preservation."

We have made this extract to show that, by inserting the word "*white*" it was distinctly designed to exclude "negroes" or "coloured people" from the right to vote. The Report was discussed by Mr. RENSELLAER, Mr. FAIRLIE, Mr. YOUNG, Mr. ROOT, Mr. CLARKE and others.

After much debate, Mr. Jay, who is now at the head of the abolitionists in New York, moved to strike out the word "white," the effect of which would be to admit *all persons, black or white*, possessed of certain other qualifications, to the exercise of the right of suffrage. In opposing this measure, Chief Justice Spencer said—

"I have believed, and do still believe, that we are called on to extend the right of suffrage as far as the interests of the community will permit; but I do think we cannot contemplate carrying it to the full extent recommended in the report, without knowing that we are not giving to those people who

Van Buren's Negro Voters !

"*Stan bak, you poor white trash ; you got no property—we gemmen ob color voies fur Missa Van Buren and Missa Johnson ; dey is de color friends and feller-citizens : Missa Van Burn he mend de constushon ob de York state to let we gemmen ob color vote, case we got $250, so you poor white bog-trotters and clod-hoppers stan back.*"

"*Massa Van Buren's frens wen dey men de Merland constushon vell please member to gib our bre'ren dere rights same as Missa Van Buren gib us in de York state.*"

will nominally enjoy the right, but to those who feed and clothe them. I shall vote against striking out the word white, on the ground that it is necessary for securing our own happiness."

The question on striking out the word *white, (which would give all, whether black or white, the privilege of voting, if possessed of a certain amount of property,)* was then taken by ayes and noes, and decided in the affirmative, as follows :

AYES—Messrs. Bacon, Baker, Barlow, Beckwith, Birdseye, Brinkerhoff, Brooks, Buel, Burroughs, Carver, R. Clark, Collins, Cramer, Day, Dodge, Duer, Eastwood, Edwards, Ferris, Fish, Hallock, Hees, Hogeboom, Hunting, Huntington, Jay, Jones, Kent, King, Moore, Munro, Nelson, Park, Paulding, Pitcher, Platt, Reeve, Rhinelander, Richards, Rodgers, Roseburgh, Sanders, N. Sanford, Seaman, Steele, D. Sutherland, Swift, Sylvester, Tallmadge, Tuttle, VAN BUREN, Van Ness, J. R. Van Renselær, Van Vechten, Ward, A. Webster, Wendover, Wheaton, E. Williams, Woodward, Wooster, Yates—63.

NOES—Messrs. Bowman, Breese, Briggs, Carpenter, Case, Child, D. Clark, Clyde, Dubois, Dyckman, Fairlie, Fenton, Frost, Howe, Humphrey, Hunt, Hunter, Hurd, Knowles, Lansing, Lawrence, Lefferts, A. Livingston, P. R. Livingston, M'Call, Millikin, Pike, Porter, Price, Pumply, Radcliff, Rockwell, Root, Rosa, Ross, Russell, Sage, R. Sanford, Schenck, Seely, Sharpe, Sheldon, I. Smith, Spencer, Starkweather, I. Southerland, Taylor, Ten Eyck, Townley, Townsend, Tripp, Van Fleet, Van Horne, Verbryck, E. Webster, Wheeler, Woods, Young—59."

☞ We here see that Mr. Van Buren voted to strike out the word WHITE, so as to give the NEGRO the right of voting.

United States of America,
STATE OF MARYLAND, TO WIT:

I, Jas. B. Latimer, Notary Public in and for the city of Baltimore, do hereby certify, that I have carefully examined and compared the above extract, as printed, with the original on page 202, of the volume entitled "Reports of the Proceedings and Debates of the Convention of 1821, assembled for the purpose of amending the constitution of New York," and find the same to agree with said original in all particulars.

{SEAL.} In witness whereof, I have hereunto set my hand and affixed my notarial seal, on this eleventh day of August, 1836.

JAMES B. LATIMER.
Notary Public.

☞ In the same Convention, (see Journal of Proceedings, pages 277, 283 and 284,) Mr. Van Buren opposed the poor man's voting if he did not own a certain amount of property [$250 worth] or paid taxes, or worked on the highways. See Mr. Van Buren's speech :

The question before the convention was to strike out the provision requiring a property qualification to entitle a man to vote :

Mr. Van Buren felt himself called upon to make a few remarks in reply to the gentleman from Delaware county, (Mr. Root.) He observed that it was evident, and indeed some gentlemen did not seem to disguise it, that the amendment proposed contemplated *nothing short* of *universal suffrage*. Mr. Van Buren did not believe that there

were twenty members of that committee, who, were the bare naked question of universal suffrage put to them, would vote in its favor; and he was very sure that its adoption was not expected, and would not meet the views of their constituents." Again he says,

"One word on the main question before the committee. We had already reached the verge of Universal Suffrage. There was but one step beyond, and are gentlemen prepared to take that ? We were *cheapening this invaluable right.* He was disposed to go as far as any in the extension of rational liberty, but he could not consent to undervalue this precious privilege so far as to confer it with an indiscriminating hand upon every one."—That is, if a white or a *black* man owns $250, he is to enjoy this precious privilege !

Again—Mr. Van Buren spoke against the amendment and against Universal Suffrage.

RED-BAITING,
FLAG-WAVING, AND
OTHER FEATS OF
DEMAGOGUERY

BY THE SKIN OF HIS TEETH?

Candidates' concern with image started with George Washington. Although his skin was bad, the Founding Father was more worried about the discomfort and appearance problems caused by his teeth. He began using false teeth in the election year of 1789, as a campaign device. Years later, he had a second set made of ivory, but those were effectively useless for eating.

"Politics makes me sick."
> —WILLIAM HOWARD TAFT, BEFORE BEING NOMINATED
> FOR THE PRESIDENCY BY THE REPUBLICAN PARTY. HE
> MANAGED TO FIGHT BACK HIS NAUSEA UPON HIS
> ELECTION.

THIS CAMPAIGN ISN'T SUPPOSED TO BE A JOKE

With both parties beseeching the robber barons of American industry for contributions to purchase the "floating vote," thugs acting as ballot box stuffers, and the two presidential candidates (Grover Cleveland and James Blaine) accused of every sort of moral and financial turpitude, it's no wonder that foreign journalists looked upon the election of 1884 as though it was being conducted on another planet.

The distinguished Henry Adams obviously thought that the situation had degenerated to the risible when he wrote to a friend in England:

> We are plunged into politics funnier than words can
> express. Very great issues are involved . . . We are all
> doing our best, swearing at each other like demons. But

the amusing thing is that *no one talks about real
interests. By common consent they agree to let these
alone. We are afraid to discuss them.* Instead of this the
press is engaged in a most amusing dispute whether Mr.
Cleveland had an illegitimate child, or did or did not live
with more than one mistress; whether Mr. Blaine got paid
in railway bonds for his work as Speaker . . . I have
laughed myself red with amusement over the letters,
affidavits, leading articles and speeches which are flying
through the air. Society is torn to pieces. Parties are
wrecked from top to bottom. A great political revolution
is impending. Yet, when I am not angry, I can do
nothing but laugh.

Quick now, was that 1884, or 1984?

A CAMPAIGN SLUR BACKFIRES

The presidential election of 1884 is properly remembered as one
of the dirtiest in history. But the outcome may have turned upon
a little-noticed incident involving political spying, which helped
transform a possible election winner into an all-but-forgotten
loser.

Strangely enough, the ultimate victor was the candidate remembered as the victim of scandalmongers. Grover Cleveland,
the Democratic nominee, had served only one term as governor
of New York and was relatively unknown. He became the subject
of crude campaign jokes and bawdy derision, when a Buffalo
newspaper made it known that he'd had an affair with a young
widow and supposedly fathered a child, while refusing to marry
her.

Actually, as writer John M. Taylor has pointed out, Cleveland
had provided financial support for the child, despite nagging
questions concerning whether or not he actually was the father.
And, to his credit, Cleveland didn't hide the past relationship,
even when faced with cruel campaign taunts of "Ma, ma, where's
my pa? Gone to the White House, ha, ha, ha!''

However, it was the beloved, charismatic Republican candidate, James G. Blaine, the "Plumed Knight" of American politics, who was better known. Reeling from the Cleveland paternity scandal, the Democrats attacked Blaine viciously, effectively portraying the GOP nominee as the vassal of the influence-peddling railroad lobby, a charge not without substance.

When Republican power brokers found themselves behind in the polls, they convinced Blaine, a stirring stump speaker, to undertake a last-ditch, whistle-stop train campaign through the Northeast and Midwest. When their standard-bearer was warmly received by crowds of rich and poor alike, the come-from-behind strategy was thought to be working beautifully, until an exhausted Blaine agreed to one last stop in New York City for an eleventh-hour fund-raiser.

What was to be a routine testimonial by Protestant clergymen supporting the Republican ticket turned into disaster. The minister scheduled to keynote the speakers' program was delayed, and as his replacement the clergymen chose the Reverend Samuel Burchard, of the Murray Hill Presbyterian Church. Evidently no one at the meeting had heard the flamboyant Rev. Burchard speak before.

"We are Republicans," Burchard thundered during his endorsement, "and don't propose to leave our party and identify ourselves with the party whose antecedents have been rum, Romanism and rebellion."

Apparently not comprehending the nasty political and religious implications of the minister's oath of political fealty, Blaine offered his thanks and little other comment, and the show was over.

Or, was it? The significance of Burchard's slur against the Roman Catholic church was not lost on the Democratic spies, or "trailers" as they were then called. By the time they got through spreading the word about the controversial remark, many Catholics believed that Blaine himself had uttered the condemnation, and "rum, Romanism and rebellion" quickly became a campaign slogan—for the other side.

The Democrats subsequently carried New York and all its

critical electoral votes by a narrow 1,200-vote margin. It seems likely that Burchard's last-minute, off the cuff attack relegated Blaine to history and helped elevate the scandal-tarred Cleveland to the White House, where he served two non-consecutive terms.

BILEFUL BILBO

Mississippi senator Theodore "the Man" Bilbo was a piece of work. A Southern demagogue who was almost a caricature of the scheming, corrupt politician, Bilbo specialized in rabble-rousing and ugly, personal attacks on his political rivals. In one of his earliest campaigns, for example, he described his opponent as a "cross between a hyena and a mongrel . . . begotten in a nigger graveyard at midnight, suckled by a sow, and educated by a fool." Not shockingly, the target of his invective searched him out, and beat him into an unconsciousness that lasted twenty-four hours.

That didn't deter the man editor J. T. Salter called "The Old Maestro of the Stump." In his 1915 gubernatorial campaign, here's what Bilbo had to say about his opponent: "John Armstrong is a vicious, deliberate, cowardly, pusillanimous, cold-blooded, lop-eared, blue-nosed, pre-meditated, and self-made liar." Almost twenty years later, Bilbo's foes learned that time had not mellowed the Mississippi malefactor: "Hubert Stevens," Bilbo said of his state's incumbent senator, "is a . . . plain United States Senatorial liar."

During a campaign in 1934, Bilbo unleashed just a bit of the crowd-pleasing style that delighted his backwoods supporters in the Depression-era Delta region: "My opponent—yea, this opponent of mine who has the dastardly, dew-lapped, brazen, sneering, insulting and sinful effrontery to ask you for your votes without telling you, the people of this almighty state of Mississippi what he is a-going to do with them if he gets them—this opponent of mine says he don't need a platform."

Mightily impressed with his own bloviating, Bilbo continued: "The appeal and petition of the humblest citizen, yea, whether he comes from the black prairie lands of the east or the alluvial hills of north Mississippi or the sun-kissed shores of the Gulf of Mexico, yea, he will be heard by my heart and my feet shall be swift."

Unfortunately the voters were impressed and sent this fraud to the U.S. Senate.

JUST A LITTLE RACE-BAITING

While historians have been tough on the inept administration of President Warren Harding and his corrupt "Ohio Gang" of influence-peddlers, the distinguished-looking former newspaper editor-turned-politician really was a pretty nice guy who tried to be a good chief executive and wanted to please just about everyone. One of his more admirable qualities was his personal empathy for those unfortunates who were ostracized because of some abnormality in their appearance. The young Harding had suffered through such indignities as a child, when despite his handsome features, he was called "the little nigger" by schoolmates and others because of the dark, swarthy tone of his skin and his jet-black hair.

This childhood taunt was cruelly revived by a college professor, William E. Chancellor of Wooster College, who published circulars claiming that Harding possessed Negro blood. In the climactic weeks of the 1920 election, the rumors about the Republican candidate's allegedly mixed ancestry were revived, but many newspapers refused to print the slurs, and to their credit, the Democrats decided to ignore the issue.

FIGHTING BOB

U.S. Senator Robert LaFollette of Wisconsin became the candidate of the third party Conference for Progressive Political Action (CPPA) in 1924 when Democrat William McAdoo was publicly linked with the Teapot Dome scandal (John Davis finally became the Democrats' compromise choice when they couldn't decide between McAdoo and New York governor Al Smith). "Fighting Bob" certainly had the credentials and the crusading spirit to lead the progressives, but his candidacy came at the wrong time, both politically and economically.

Democratic and Republican local workers did all they could to discourage the Progressives; their rallies were repeatedly broken up for "disturbing the peace." The "Red Scare" of 1919–20 caused LaFollette to be labeled a "Bolshevik" by nervous conservatives worried about the recent Communist revolution in Russia.

Coolidge's soothing refrain, "The business of America is business" drew the corporate moguls to his side, and many workers were bluntly told not to bother to return to work if Cautious Cal lost the election. Bankers warned farmers inclined to support the populist senator that their loans might be in danger if Coolidge wasn't reelected to the White House. Nevertheless, LaFollette managed to gain almost five million votes as a third party candidate.

THE (UN)HAPPY WARRIOR

The burning question of the 1928 presidential campaign was whether a Roman Catholic could be elected president of the United States. Carrying that unwelcome burden for the Democrats was the Tammany-bred, self-educated governor of New York, Al Smith. Dubbed "The Happy Warrior" by Franklin Roosevelt, Smith won the nomination after failing to gain it in 1924 because of a stubborn deadlock between him and Woodrow Wilson's son-in-law, William McAdoo. (John Davis was chosen as a compromise candidate after more than a hundred ballots; he was given a thrashing by Cal Coolidge and became a footnote to political history.)

Smith's Catholic faith wasn't his only Achilles' heel; as a "Wet," he also favored the repeal of Prohibition, not a popular sentiment in the South and West. Although he didn't necessarily share these views, Oswald G. Villard, owner and editor of *The Nation*, pretty well summed up Smith's political baggage with these derogatory estimates:

Would you vote for a Tammany Hall roughneck like
"Al" Smith? Would you have Al spitting tobacco juice
about in the White House as he does in the Governor's
room at Albany? Do you believe in electing to the
Presidency a man who drinks too much for his own
good? . . . Would you vote for a Catholic in the White
House? Do you believe in having as President a man who
boasts that he has never read a book?

Smith's candidacy opened the floodgates for some of the worst
religious bigotry since the heyday of the anti-Catholic, anti-
immigrant Know-Nothings of the mid-nineteenth century. The
then-powerful Ku Klux Klan launched a "Klarion Kall for a
Crusade" to keep Smith from being elected, and many Protes-
tants joined in the vulgar propaganda attack. Klansmen in Indiana
warned voters to "watch the trains," as the much-feared pope
could be coming in person to bless the Smith campaign.

"No Governor can kiss the Papal ring and get within gunshot
of the White House," pledged Methodist bishop Adna Leonard.
Rumors were circulated that Catholics took a secret oath to fight
Protestantism, and the worst kind of outrageous horror stories
made the rounds about alleged sexual indignities suffered by
ex-nuns. Smith even received loads of anti-Catholic tracts at his
home, some of them pornographic.

An effective, well-organized whispering campaign was aimed
at the governor. It was falsely said that Smith only appointed Catholics and Jews to state office, and his Tammany patronage background made that charge difficult to refute. Stories repeatedly
cropped up that Smith was constantly drunk in public; all of the
anecdotes had the common theme that it "took two men" to hold
him up. One prominent Republican woman attacked him as a
"rum-soaked Romanist," and Coolidge Justice Department official Mabel Willebrandt actually went on the campaign stump,
blasting Smith's Tammany links and his stand against Prohibition.

Kansas editor William Allen White, influential in the Midwest
and supposedly a Smith admirer, attacked the candidate for his

votes in favor of liquor sales and for not doing more to crack down on gambling and prostitution. "Tammany is indeed Tammany," White concluded in a series of broadsides that stunned and enraged the Democratic standard-bearer.

Smith's opponent, Republican Herbert Hoover, a veteran public servant, was denigrated for his Quaker background, and claimed the slanders against both men cancelled each other out. But the criticisms of him were minor and politically inconsequential compared to the volume and viciousness of the assaults loosed on Smith. "I was probably the outstanding victim of the last half century of a whispering campaign," lamented the Happy Warrior after his almost inevitable defeat.

He tried unsuccessfully for the nomination a third time in 1932, but his moment had passed. It would be thirty-two years before a younger, more attractive Catholic candidate, John F. Kennedy, would overcome the religious bigotry that hounded Smith, and win the White House.

A REAL ELECTION FIGHT

Most who knew him as Speaker of the House realized that Texas congressman Jim Wright was a pugnacious politician who gave a blow for every one received. Perhaps only the residents of his Fort Worth district knew, however, just how handy and eager the bantamweight Wright was with his fists. As a young office-seeker, he literally may have punched his way into the state legislature, as he related to writer Thomas Edsall years after the incident.

Right after World War II, as a twenty-two-year-old liberal shaking hands for votes at an American Legion breakfast, he was called a sissy and "a Commie sonofabitch" by a local trouble-maker who may already have had a few stiff eye-openers with his eggs. The malefactor, who Wright said was named Dub Tucker, then decided to swing a haymaker in the would-be politician's direction. Seeing the roundhouse coming, Wright rolled with it, "dug my left fist as hard as I could into his ample midriff, and then my right," before hitting his critic half a dozen more times, after which he "crumpled like a sack of wet laundry."

Far from outraging the local citizenry, the morning slugfest "may have been the best thing that happened in my race for the legislature" that year, Wright recalled years later. Those suspicious of his views were heartened by the sight of his willingness to provide his critics with a knuckle sandwich.

STREET FIGHTING MAN

A hot-tempered ex-marine who never shied away from political controversy or a fight, the patrician-looking Richardson Dilworth was what one Philadelphia reporter called a "slam bang campaigner." Throughout his long career of public service, which included jobs ranging from city treasurer to mayor, the feisty Dilworth called them as he saw them in the City of Brotherly Love. His specialty was the street corner rally, which he developed into an art form in the mid-1950s.

Using a local Democratic band as a warm-up, Dilworth toured neighborhoods in a sound truck, issuing amplified denunciations of what he considered the pervasive corruption of the Republican administration. Once, according to writer Sam Smith, who stuffed envelopes for Dilworth's campaigns, the candidate parked next to the mayor's home and told a surprised audience: "Over here across the street is a house of prostitution and a numbers bank. And just a few doors further down on this side of the street is the district police station. . . . The only reason the GOP district czars let Bernard Samuel stay on as mayor is that he lets them do just as they please."

Dilworth's family also enjoyed playing backup for the activist head of their household. On one occasion, his wife knocked a heckler off the platform with her handbag. His daughter picketed the office of her dad's mayoral opponent, W. Thatcher Longstreth, with a sign proclaiming: "Mr. Longstreth, why won't you debate the issues with my father on TV?"

Another time, when the local GOP city chairman, William

Meade, denounced the Americans for Democratic Action (ADA), of which Dilworth was a member, as being "inside pink" and full of communists, Dilworth furiously called Meade a "liar." Then he charged into Meade's office, demanding that the accuser produce evidence of his smear. Dilworth threw down the challenge "as one who fought for his country in the Marine Corps. That's more than you did, Mr. Meade."

"Maybe I wasn't physically fit," Meade replied, rather lamely.

Dilworth was elected mayor in 1955 and continued his bully-bashing, which included numerous feuds with another legendary street fighter, police chief and mayor Frank Rizzo, until his death in 1974.

THE KKK'S MAN

The 1946 gubernatorial race in Georgia was a field day for race-baiters, and the unchallenged champion of race politics that year was the "man from Sugar Creek," Eugene Talmadge, an ex-governor of the state seeking a return to office. Campaigning in his trademark red galluses, or suspenders, Talmadge delighted his fans in the hate-mongering Ku Klux Klan with his bold pronouncements of white supremacy.

The Exalted Cyclops of "Klavern No. 297" excitedly reported that if their man Talmadge was elected, the KKK would have a big influence in getting their members into police jobs, and in handling "Negro parades." On another occasion, the Cyclops reportedly asked his favorite candidate's sage advice for dealing with race problems. Talmadge didn't answer, according to crusading liberal columnist Drew Pearson, but instead picked up a pencil and paper and wrote, "pistols."

When the Supreme Court ruled that blacks had the right to vote in Democratic primaries, old Gene came up with a crowd-pleasing plan to run a private primary administered by his own political organization. The enlightened Talmadge's reading material included Hitler's *Mein Kampf*, which the politician claimed to have read seven times.

In a clever ploy to smear his primary opponent, James Carmichael, Talmadge hired a Carmichael look-alike to drive around the state greeting voters from a limousine, with two blacks puffing cigars in the backseat. Despite (or perhaps because of) his reactionary appeal, Talmadge lost the popular vote, but won on the state's "unit rule" system. He died in December 1946 before he could take office.

DAVY CROCKETT'S STAND-IN

Few outside their home state of Tennessee could see much of a connection between rugged frontier legend Davy Crockett and the professorial-looking Senator Estes Kefauver, the leader of several Capitol Hill probes into organized crime. But a coonskin cap made both famous, for different reasons.

In 1948, when Kefauver began his campaign for the Senate against Republican Tom Stewart, political boss Ed Crump, a Stewart booster, sneeringly called the Democrat the "Communists' pet coon." Although possessed of a solemn manner and dignified appearance, Kefauver responded by showing he had a sense of humor. At a speech before several hundred voters, he said, "I know one thing, I'm not Mr. Crump's pet coon."

Then, amid much laughter, he pulled out a large, furry coonskin cap and proceeded to wear it throughout the campaign as a victory hat. He won handily.

THE RED PEPPER CAMPAIGN

While it may be difficult to single out one Senate election race as the dirtiest in history, the 1950 campaign between Florida's accomplished incumbent, Claude Pepper, and his opponent, George Smathers, wins a special place in the mudslingers' hall of fame. Smathers, who once had been a protégé of the older Pepper, cleverly milked voter ignorance and fear to grossly distort his former mentor's record and character—and the brazen assault catapulted him into the Senate.

Capitalizing on the comparatively low literacy level among

Florida's rural voters, Smathers's backers successfully attacked Pepper with a series of damaging malapropisms, including:

—"Pepper is known all over Washington as a shameless *extrovert!*"

—"Pepper has a sister who was once a *thespian!*"

—"Pepper practiced *celibacy* before his marriage!"

Race also became a useful weapon. A black janitor was paid to approach Pepper, grab his hand, and hold it until the camera light flashed, so that the candidate would be pictured on the front page of the local newspaper shaking hands with a black supporter, a kiss of political death in then-segregationist Florida. "That hurt," Pepper recalled to political columnist Christopher Matthews nearly forty years later.

The crushing blow of the campaign was the false charge that Pepper was a Bolshevik sympathizer. His attackers distributed a McCarthy-like pamphlet entitled "The Red Record of Senator Pepper," detailing his supposedly communist views.

Pepper's failure to rebut the phony charges led to his becoming one of seven U.S. senators defeated for reelection that year. Smathers, a suave ladies' man and ardent partygoer, swaggered into the Senate and became a friend and drinking buddy of another handsome Washington politician and skirt-chaser, Senator John F. Kennedy.

Later elected to the House of Representatives, Pepper was respectfully addressed as "Senator" by his colleagues and staff until his death in 1990.

JERRY AND THE "PINK LADY"

Red-baiting wasn't invented by Richard Nixon, but he cleverly and ruthlessly utilized communist scare tactics to gain election to both the House in 1946 and the Senate in 1950. Despite the legitimate national security concerns of the cold war, the young Nixon labored tirelessly to effectively and inaccurately smear his opponents as eager communist sympathizers.

As a thirty-three-year-old Republican challenger to Democrat

Jerry Voorhis in California's 12th District, political novice Nixon misleadingly linked Voorhis's voting record to "communist-dominated" political action committees. He was helped by the willing assistance of the congressional district's Republican-controlled newspapers, whose owners and editors liked the newcomer's aggressiveness and pro-business message. One advertisement stated "A Vote For Nixon Is A Vote Against the Communist-Dominated PAC With Its Gigantic Slush Fund."

Nixon biographer Fawn Brodie related that one woman had told Democratic supporters of Voorhis that she had been paid nine dollars a day to anonymously call registered Democrats in the final days of the campaign and say, "Did you know that Jerry Voorhis is a communist," before abruptly hanging up. Nixon also accused Voorhis of only passing one bill in four years, and that legislation "adopted transferred activities concerning rabbits from one federal department to another." Nixon won handily over an opponent who didn't know what had hit him until long after he'd been ousted from Congress. In fact, Voorhis couldn't even bring himself to speak or write of Richard Nixon until a quarter century had passed.

Four years later, after gaining national recognition as one of the chief accusers of alleged communist spy Alger Hiss, Nixon saw a golden opportunity to move up to the Senate when a woman he saw as vulnerable, Democratic congresswoman Helen Gahagan Douglas, gained her party's nomination to run. "There will be no name-calling, no smears, no misrepresentation in this campaign," pledged Nixon.

Right—and the check's in the mail. Nixon went after the liberal Douglas, a former opera singer and the wife of well-known Hollywood actor Melvyn Douglas, with a fury. Labeling her "the pink lady," Nixon linked Douglas's voting record, in what became popularly known as the "pink sheet," to that of her fellow legislator, New York congressman Vito Marcantonio, who adhered to the "notorious Communist party line," according to the Republican candidate. Mrs. Douglas was "pink right down to her underwear," Nixon said.

In a rather ill-advised move, the opinionated congresswoman got right down in the dirt with her accuser. Calling Nixon and his supporters "a backwash of men in dark shirts," and thus bluntly comparing them to fascists, she overreacted and blasted Nixon with a rejoinder called "The Big Lie . . . Hitler invented it—Stalin perfected it—Nixon uses it."

The mudslinging ended with a decisive, 600,000-vote victory by Nixon, but Mrs. Douglas may have had the last laugh. Seizing upon a descriptive phrase about her tormentor from an editorial, she repeated it until it became part of the popular lexicon of epithets about Nixon: "Tricky Dick."

FREE FOR ALL

In the 1952 presidential campaign, the Democrats faced an almost insurmountable problem—the "Ike factor." Dwight Eisenhower, the heroic commander of America's victorious forces in Europe during World War II, had been courted by both parties to head their presidential tickets. Personally attacking the immensely popular general, who then had no political record, was almost out of the question. His running mate, Senator Richard Nixon, despite his relative youth, had plenty of enemies due to his successful use of Communist-baiting tactics against his opponents, and he became the focus of one of the worst mudslinging campaigns of the century.

SECRET NIXON FUND!, a banner headline in the *New York Post* of September 18 in the midst of the campaign, drew national attention to a charge that threatened Nixon's position on the Republican ticket: that he had drawn living expenses from a fund of $18,000 donated by dozens of private businessmen in his home state of California. While high-living wasn't among Nixon's sins, his sanctimonious explanations didn't stop the Democrats from labeling the fund as "bribery"; several influential newspapers called for him to quit the ticket.

President Truman, who detested Nixon, ordered his attorney general to launch a criminal investigation of the informal fund. Eisenhower, whose political weather vane was more sensitive than most realized, waited on the sidelines to see which way the wind would blow for his vice-presidential candidate.

Although it was still the dawn of the television age, Nixon saved his place on the ticket, and his political career, with a maudlin, but highly effective speech seen by almost sixty million American viewers. In what was forever memorialized as the "Checkers" speech, Nixon gave an earnest but rather corny defense of his actions, denying that he'd benefited from the businessmen's fund, but admitting that he had kept one gift from a supporter—a cocker spaniel sent by an admirer in Texas.

"And our little girl—Tricia, the six year old—named it Checkers. And you know the kids love that dog and I just want to say this right now, that regardless of what they say about it, we're going to keep it."

While many viewers found the speech transparently manipulative, if not downright sickening, it forced a somewhat reluctant Eisenhower to declare his loyalty to Nixon. However, the scent of blood just made the desperate Democrats even more eager to use Nixon to get at the seemingly untouchable Eisenhower. During the final six weeks of the campaign, a number of stories, many erroneous, were published concerning Nixon's taxes and supposedly profligate spending habits.

As Professor Steven Ambrose noted in his definitive study of Nixon's political education, the Democratic National Committee attempted to use forged letters to show that Nixon had accepted more than $50,000 from the oil industry. The allegations were false, but that wasn't proven until after the election.

Nixon hardly was an innocent victim, though. In characteristic fashion, he lashed back at his accusers in a series of intense, emotional attacks that stunned even Republican supporters. He blasted the principled Democratic candidate, Adlai Stevenson, as a "weakling, a waster and a small caliber Truman," and all but called the distinguished if haughty Secretary of State Dean Acheson a communist.

Perhaps most disturbingly, neither Nixon nor Eisenhower put a lid on the witch-hunting tactics of Wisconsin senator Joseph McCarthy, who was then at the height of his inexplicable hold on cold war America. To his disgrace and the shock of even his close friends, Ike didn't defend fellow military hero Gen. George

Marshall from scurrilous stabs by the McCarthyites, who outrageously suggested that Marshall was disloyal.

Stevenson, the only man to come out of the flurry of namecalling with his reputation intact, was soundly defeated and forced to watch as Eisenhower carried the Republicans to a crushing victory that gave them effective control of the House and Senate.

A HIDDEN CAMPAIGN MESSAGE

Sex has played a decisive role in many American elections, but perhaps never in so bizarre a fashion than in a 1974 Virginia congressional race. One of the candidates, a young man named Dennis Gregg, claimed that his opponents, among them Democrat Joseph Fisher, "distributed campaign literature that had the word 'sex' subliminally imbedded" all over their pictures, according to an account by reporter Myra McPherson.

Since Fisher looked more like a conservatively dressed, bespectacled high school mathematics teacher than a movie star, the suggestion seemed a bit puzzling. Nevertheless, the stubborn Gregg produced a letter from a university professor that outlined how "subliminal communications techniques" affect people. "Subliminal imbeds in the form of the word 'sex' can be very lightly etched into the photographic portraits," intoned the academic missive authoritatively.

Some observers thought the earnest Gregg was kidding until he filed a complaint with the Fair Campaign Practices Committee, requesting an immediate investigation of the "unethical subliminal" methods being employed by his opponents. The voters ultimately decided that the nonsexy Fisher was good enough for them, and elected him over a longtime Republican incumbent. It's not known if Mr. Gregg went into advertising.

THE DINNERTIME DEMAGOGUE

The ugly, suspicious cold war era of "McCarthyism," which bears the name of the former, infamous junior senator from Wis-

TAKE YOUR CHOICE OF THE TWO BILLS!

consin, wasn't born of an honest ideological crusade, nor a sincere effort to protect unsuspecting Americans from ruthless totalitarian enemies abroad. Rather, the years of hysterical hunting for Communists in the government began as a campaign tool, pure and simple.

By 1950, Joe McCarthy, considerably younger and legislatively lazier than most of his peers, realized he hadn't accomplished much in the Senate and was already desperately looking for an issue to propel him to reelection in 1952. At a dinner meeting to discuss McCarthy's political future at Washington's Colony Restaurant, he and his informal board of advisers rejected one issue after another as too dull a theme upon which to promote a dynamic campaign.

"How about communism as an issue?" suggested Father Edmund Walsh, dean of the Georgetown School of Foreign Service. While McCarthy previously had used communism to smear political opponents, he'd apparently never thought of it as a potential vehicle to make him a household name. "The government is full of Communists . . . The thing to do is hammer at them."

Within thirty days, he had devised the basic outlines of the thundering, accusatory speech that would make him the primary villain and spokesman for what writer Lillian Hellman called the "scoundrel time."

THE SILVER BULLET

In an almost macabre fashion, the wounds suffered by Texas governor John Connally during the 1963 assassination of John F. Kennedy may have assured his reelection in 1964. The sympathy vote alone made him a formidable candidate, but handsome liberal activist Don Yarborough waged a tough, effective primary campaign against the still-injured Connally, who continued to wear a black sling to protect the arm through which a presidential assassin's bullet had passed in the Dallas motorcade.

As the final May vote approached, however, Connally took one simple act that many veteran political observers claimed made him unbeatable—he removed the protective coverage around his arm during a campaign speech in south Texas and revealed a renewed wholeness, which was an almost religious revelation for Texas voters. "That kills us," a perceptive Yarborough told his campaign staff, as related by Connally biographer James Reston, Jr.

Although he might have won in any event, more cynical observers claimed the "silver bullet" saved Connally's political career at the time. "He ain't never done nothing but get shot in Dallas," drawled Texas comptroller Bob Bullock years later. "He needs to come back here and get himself shot every six months."

QUOTATIONS OF AND ABOUT CHAIRMAN RIZZO

"He's certainly a Hitler. He's a typical dictator demagogue. He makes [former Alabama governor and presidential candidate] George Wallace look like an amateur. He's created a terrible atmosphere of fear in this city. He's a stupid, arrogant son of a bitch. And that's on the record."
—FORMER U.S. SENATOR AND PHILADELPHIA MAYOR
JOE CLARK, ON FELLOW DEMOCRAT FRANK RIZZO, THEN
THE PARTY'S NOMINEE FOR MAYOR./*PHILADELPHIA
EVENING BULLETIN*, OCT. 29, 1975.

"I'm going to make Attilla the Hun look like a faggot after this election's over."
—MAYORAL CANDIDATE FRANK RIZZO, COMMENTING
ON HIS FUTURE ADMINISTRATION'S LAW ENFORCEMENT
POLICIES.

"What's the big deal about lying in a bathroom?"
—MAYOR RIZZO, AFTER FAILING A LIE DETECTOR TEST
HE'D VOLUNTEERED TO TAKE IN AUGUST 1973,
CONCERNING AN ALLEGED DEAL TO SECURE THE
NOMINATION OF A DEMOCRATIC CANDIDATE FOR DISTRICT
ATTORNEY.

*"I refuse to answer, on the grounds it might tend to
incriminate me."*
—THE BUILDING CONTRACTOR AND GENERAL MANAGER
OF A CONSTRUCTION COMPANY, WHICH ADDED AN
ESTIMATED $320,000 WORTH OF ADDITIONS TO MAYOR
RIZZO'S HOME WITHOUT THE REQUIRED CITY PERMITS
AND LICENSES.

*". . . . I repeat that we have the safest city in the United
States. . . . But it's the people that make it unsafe."*
—MAYOR RIZZO, IN CAMPAIGN COMMENTS OPPOSING
MUNICIPAL NOMINEES HE CONSIDERED TOO LENIENT ON
CRIME.

"He couldn't draw flies."
—MAYOR RIZZO, DISMISSING A CAMPAIGN OPPONENT.

*"In desperate times, people turn to a demagogue. Frank
Rizzo is a demagogue."*
—DAVID BUFFINGTON, *PENNSYLVANIA REPORT*,
EXPLAINING HOW RIZZO WAS ABLE TO CAPTURE THE
REPUBLICAN NOMINATION FOR MAYOR IN 1991 AFTER
DEFECTING FROM THE DEMOCRATIC PARTY.

JIMMY CARTER'S "STINK TANK"

Former Georgia governor Jimmy Carter charmed the Democratic party and the nation with his toothy grin and the pledge that he'd never tell a lie; his informal, folksy campaign style carried him into the White House in 1976. Carter's populist appeal had a much harder edge to it, though, when he ran for governor against the Peach State's former chief executive, Carl Sanders, in 1970.

"I'm basically a redneck," Carter told a Georgia reporter during the gubernatorial campaign, in which he repeatedly referred to his opponent as "Cuff Links Carl." One of Carter's television ads showed a man wearing large cuff links disembarking from a private jet and taking a bucket of cash from another man. The former peanut farmer, although by then a wealthy man himself, portrayed Sanders as a candidate who'd gotten rich in office and was out of touch with the state's voters, according to an account by legal journalist Steven Brill.

At one point, Carter distributed a so-called "proof packet" to back his charges that Sanders had previously used his office for personal financial gain. The "list" turned out to be an unsubstantiated allegation that Sanders once had intervened at the Federal Communication Commission on behalf of a friend.

That tactic was tame compared to several other stunts the Carter team unleashed on Sanders. An anonymous leaflet was circulated that showed Sanders, once part owner of the Atlanta Hawks basketball team, being given a champagne shampoo by two of the squad's black players, as part of a victory party. Both Carter and his staff denied any connection with the pamphlet, which was designed to make Sanders look bad among Georgia's conservative white voters.

But Ralph Abernathy, an Atlanta public relations executive who worked for Carter's media director, Gerald Rafshoon, told Brill: "We distributed that leaflet . . . it was part of an operation called 'the stink tank.' " Abernathy also disclosed that Carter's campaign had also paid for the media advertising of C. B. King, a black lawyer also running for governor: the Carter camp believed that King, who had no chance of winning, would draw voters away from Sanders.

The clandestine activities contrast rather starkly with Carter's claim in his autobiography that "I don't know how to compromise on any principle."

VOTE FOR CUOMO, NOT THE HOMO

Love him or hate him, the feisty, quotable former New York City mayor Ed Koch had something to say about everything going on in the Big Apple. When he first ran for mayor in 1977, however, one of his opponents spread some not-so-nice rumors about Koch's private life. During the campaign, the *Village Voice* ran a story entitled "Smear News Is No News," which alleged that Michael Dowd, campaign manager for Mario Cuomo (now governor of New York), had hired a private detective to snoop into bachelor Koch's social life. Another Cuomo staffer, according to the story, paid a "security consultant" to determine whether "there was a chance Koch had a few boyfriends."

For his part, Cuomo was quoted as being shocked at being told of the spying. "I'm so . . . disappointed . . . What if you hurt the fellow and he wins? What you've done is you've scarred the reputation of the mayor of the greatest city in the world."

Koch wasn't buying any of his foe's claims of innocence. In his view, Cuomo had to have known what his top aides were up to, and the fact that Cuomo failed to discipline the guilty campaign workers was proof of it. Koch was further outraged when someone who didn't like him put up flyers around the city that read, "Vote For Cuomo, Not The Homo," although Cuomo's backers weren't linked to the offending posters.

For his part, the thin-skinned Cuomo insisted on an apology for a truck loudspeaker that had blared, "A vote for Cuomo is the vote for the Mafia." Koch responded that he didn't even believe that the incident had happened.

DOES THIS MEAN YOU WON'T DONATE?

In 1980, the National Conservative Political Action Committee (NCPAC), called "NicPac" for short, gave negative campaigning a new meaning when the group targeted five liberal Democratic senators for defeat in the 1980 elections. The NCPAC hit squad, headed by a young Republican firebrand named Terry Dolan, attracted unheard-of amounts of money to its cause through the direct mailing efforts of conservative fund-raising guru Richard Viguerie.

A good portion of the donations were channeled into vituperative (but highly effective) newspaper and television attack ads in the senators' home states. NCPAC's voter-oriented advertisements, stated the muckraking newsletter *Congress Probe,* "are often vicious attacks that strain even the loose ethical standards of political campaigns."

One of the fund-raising letters backfired on its congressional sponsors, however. A request for money attacking the five targeted senators, and signed by Illinois Republican representative Dan Crane, was so strongly worded that it drew this response from Sen. Walter "Dee" Huddleston of Kentucky:

"I have received a copy of your letters addressed to 'Fellow American,' in which you personally castigate five members of the Senate and then solicit funds to be used against them," Huddleston wrote to Crane. "While I frequently have opposed these members of the Senate on some of the issues you mentioned, I have never, never questioned their motives. . . . I also find the effort by NCPAC to use their distortions and half-truths to raise money for their own special interests to be crass, and I am surprised that a member of Congress would lend his name to such an effort."

Crane may not have been invited to the senator's home for dinner afterward, but NCPAC's slash-and-burn methods were effective—four of the five incumbents they went after were defeated for reelection, a shocking result that helped throw the Senate into the GOP's control for the first time in decades.

"You get up every morning and try to figure out how to humiliate my client. I get up every morning and try to figure out how to make him look good. I sleep better."
—POLITICAL CONSULTANT ROGER AILES TO A REPORTER.

THE GOP IN GAY PAREE

Requests for money from campaign organizations have been accompanied by some strange-sounding explanations; one Republican fund-raising letter in 1983, signed by the party's National Senatorial Committee's treasurer, Robert Perkins, must have raised a few eyebrows. Written on the stationery of the swank Prince de Galles Hotel in Paris, Perkins's letter, a copy of which was slipped to reporter Tony Capaccio, opened with the language of a trapped war correspondent's cable:

"As I write this letter to you, I imagine my eyes still burning from the clouds of tear gas that seem to be a regular occurrence in the beleaguered city of Paris, France." Gay Paree under the nation's Socialist government, according to the alarming view of Perkins, had been reduced to a "catastrophe that might one day happen at home."

"For example," continued Perkins in a breathless style, "anyone wanting to leave France can take only the equivalent of $480 in French currency with him. Imagine trying to take a vacation with your family, or a business trip, with only $480 in your pocket." Imagine! That sum might not have covered Perkins's room service tab for a week at the elegant hotel, located just off the Champs-Elysées.

"I know France is a long way away," Perkins concluded in his missive, "and it's hard to imagine the same nightmare occurring in the United States . . . [But] it's a chance we can't afford to take. Won't you sit down right now and send a check for $25?"

SEARCH AND DESTROY

The 1984 Senate race between Republican incumbent Jesse Helms and Democratic governor Jim Hunt was an all-out, take-no-prisoners slugfest that *Newsweek* magazine called "the most colorful, expensive and nasty Senate contest in the country" that election year. Fans of political bloodletting were not disappointed.

Calling his opponent a "windshield wiper" candidate—"first one way, then the other," the bespectacled Helms unleashed a series of campaign broadsides against the popular Hunt, which sharply contrasted with the senator's gentlemanly, almost courtly personal manners. Labeling Hunt as a "limousine liberal" was about the mildest charge Helms leveled. Claiming that homosexuals "have drawn a bull-eye on my campaign," Helms signed a fund-raising letter that stated: "Make no mistake: The so-called gay-rights crowd has the cash to bankroll my opponent."

Although Helms's campaign didn't sanction the attack, his supporters hardly could have been surprised when a self-described "redneck" editor named Bob Windsor published allegations in his tabloid *Landmark* that Hunt had "a lover who was a pretty young boy in college," and "a girlfriend in his office." An enthusiastic supporter of Senator Helms, Windsor added that the male student "lover" was an employee of the State Department, and that the girlfriend was a "former high-priced call girl used by the banks and big companies in Winston-Salem to entertain their guests." Hunt blasted the reports as "scurrilous lies and slander." A later retraction didn't counteract all the damaging publicity the wild charges had attracted throughout the state.

Not exactly bashful himself when it came to hitting below the belt, Hunt charged that the arch-conservative Helms was too friendly with a controversial right-wing Salvadorean political figure who'd been linked to death squads in his country. Helms dismissed Hunt's return fire by suggesting that the governor "install a WATS line for listeners to learn the 'falsehood of the day' "; he also linked the governor with "labor union bosses" and "crooks."

Blasting Helms for alleged campaign irregularities, Hunt rejoined, "Jesse says, 'If it ain't broke, don't fix it.' I say to Jesse, 'If it ain't crooked, don't hide it.' "

"What began as an ideological crusade for both sides," intoned the *Wall Street Journal,* ended "more as one long personal mission of search and destroy." North Carolina's disgusted but highly entertained voters gave Helms a narrow victory on points in the bare-knuckles political brawl, 52 percent to 48.

ONE OF THE BOYS

"We tried to kick a little ass last night."
—VICE-PRESIDENT GEORGE BUSH, BOASTING TO A GROUP
OF LONGSHOREMEN IN ELIZABETH, NEW JERSEY, THE
DAY AFTER HIS DEBATE WITH DEMOCRATIC
VICE-PRESIDENTIAL NOMINEE GERALDINE FERRARO.

A PLAGUE ON BOTH YOUR HOUSES

When veteran Republican legislator Dick Cheney left Wyoming's congressional delegation in order to become George Bush's secretary of defense, GOP strategists scrambled to hold on to the state's only House seat, and quickly brought the party's top headhunters to back their replacement candidate, Craig Thomas. Political heavy-hitters, such as National Republican Committee chairman Ed Rollins, gave the Thomas race a special priority. "GOP insiders" were quoted in published accounts as saying that there was a major effort to "dig up ammunition to use against the Democratic candidate."

Their target, John Vinich, wasn't backing off himself. He launched a series of tough, controversial campaign ads that accused Thomas of being soft on crime. One local newspaper editorialized that the advertisements were "in the gutter," but the fiesty Vinich refused demands from prominent Republicans to

ROSIE IN SQUANDERLAND

(*With apologies to Lewis Carroll, and Sir John Tenniel*)

DRAMATIS PERSONNÆ

ALICE (Rosie)	*Franklin D. Roosevelt*	KNAVE	. . . . .	*James Farley*
HATTER	*Felix Frankfurter*	KING	. . . . .	*Harry Hopkins*
MARCH HARE . .	*Henry Wallace*	QUEEN	. . . . .	*Harold Ickes*
DUCHESS	*Mrs. Franklin D. Roosevelt*	DORMOUSE	. . . .	*The Taxpayer*

pull the spots. The election contest went downhill from there. Local Democrats were outraged when Vinich was hung in effigy at a Republican campaign barbecue. The hanged figure was supposed to be a decoration for a "chuckwagon" picnic motif, and an "overzealous" campaign worker had added red suspenders to make it resemble Vinich's distinctive style of dress, according to Thomas's embarrassed supporters, who swore they had nothing to do with the tasteless prank.

Soon afterward, Vinich's detractors were at it again, questioning his veracity concerning a car accident that put the candidate in the hospital for a week. A poll question posed by the Republicans suggested that Vinich had lied about reporting that there were only two people in the car, and hinted instead that a third person, either a Democratic national committee staff member, or a "union boss from the East" was mysteriously present at the scene. "To use those kinds of tactics is unbelievable . . . Craig should try to regain control of his campaign," retorted an angry Vinich.

Finally, at least a couple of journalists covering the campaign reached their limit. "The acid of negative campaigning—an evil lately imported with new force by Republican and Democratic national campaign committees—distorts the candidates and the Wyoming political process beyond recognition," editorialized the *Casper Star-Tribune,* the largest newspaper in Wyoming.

The "assassination politics" practiced by Thomas and Vinich caused the paper to endorse a third party "fringe" candidate, Libertarian Craig McCune, who had little realistic chance of winning, but hadn't become tarred with the dirt being kicked up by the other two hopefuls. "Voters can see to it that politicians do not profit from sleaze . . . The dirtiest campaigner should lose."

Whether or not he won that unenviable title, Thomas was elected.

C-SPANNED

The creation of the cable television channel C-Span, which broadcasts congressional hearings and Washington functions to a national audience, spawned a new breed of video electioneering. In its first few years of operation, a small group of conservative Republicans first saw the network's value as a campaign tool.

Georgia congressman Newt Gingrich realized that he could take advantage of the network during the House's "special orders" period, when members gave long-winded speeches that were rarely noticed, until television cameras were allowed inside Congress. Gingrich enlisted fellow Republican conservatives Robert Walker of Pennsylvania and Vin Weber of Minnesota; they took turns preaching Reaganism and trying to pick a televised fight with the Democrats. Since the cameras were initially not permitted to pan around the floor, the television audience was unaware that often Gingrich and his cohorts were speaking to an empty gallery.

A few months before the 1984 elections, Gingrich's hard-charging bunch used their time to read a scathing report by the Republican Study Committee, blasting the foreign policy records of at least fifty House Democrats by name, all but accusing them of cowardice in everything from the Vietnam War to U.S. policy in Latin America.

Outraged, House Speaker Tip O'Neill denounced the activist conservatives and charged that their presentation was a "sham . . . for home consumption"—which, of course, it was. Shrugging off charges that his tactics smacked of McCarthyism, Gingrich demanded the right of reply and suckered the speaker into a confrontation. Trembling with anger, O'Neill called Gingrich's televised attack "the lowest thing I've seen in my thirty-two years in Congress."

It quickly became apparent that the speaker had been outfoxed. Republicans immediately demanded that O'Neill's outburst be taken down by the parliamentarian, for a formal ruling on whether O'Neill's intensely personal rebuttal had been out of order in the House's artificially polite decorum. Embarrassingly for the Democrats, Rep. Joe Moakley of Massachusetts, one of O'Neill's closest friends and allies, was in the chair and had to rule O'Neill out of order. The imbroglio made headlines and the evening news, and the tiny band of conservative firebrands had the pre-election fight they'd so carefully plotted.

NEWT-SPEAK

Flamboyant Georgia Rep. Newt Gingrich, the darling of his party's conservative wing, is a master media manipulator. He also knows how to turn political dross into gold; the trick is in how you compare your positions to those of your opponent's.

A Republican committee called "GOPAC" distributed a brochure to help Gingrich "wanna-be's" better understand how to turn the tables on their political enemies. For example, Newt's followers are for "workfare"; their opponents want "welfare." Gingrich's stands on the issues are "moral," while his detractors are "permissive." True conservative believers are on a "crusade," while liberal crybabies are wallowing in "crisis." Always describe yourself as an "activist," and your opponent as a "radical." In 'Newtspeak' you're "pro-" while the other side is "anti-."

Any questions?

THE DUKE WAS DIRTIER?

Most casual observers of the 1988 presidential race conceded the Negative Campaign Award to George Bush. Wrong answer, says University of Oklahoma professor Julian Kanter, who's studied political commercials for more than thirty years. Proportionately, the Michael Dukakis camp produced more negative ads than the Bush campaign, claims Kanter, who is curator of the University's Political Commercial Archive. The trouble was that the Democrats' commercials, starring the earnest but wooden "Duke," weren't very good, and they didn't make much of an impact on voters.

At the same time, the Bush ads, such as the infamous commercials featuring Dukakis-furloughed inmate and convicted rapist Willie Horton, were "stronger, better and more memorable" than those produced by the Massachusetts governor's advisers, according to Kanter. Also, Dukakis helped short-circuit his own campaign by repeatedly refusing to approve timely rebuttals to Bush's scathing, televised attack ads on key issues such as crime and the environment.

Neither candidate "did much to inform or enthuse" the public, concluded Kanter. He added that, in his view, the political commercials aired during the Bush/Dukakis slugfest were "the most negative since 1964," when Lyndon Johnson's handlers stirred up a political "mini-drama" by employing new, creative video techniques to effectively question Senator Barry Goldwater's fitness for the presidency.

HELMS'S HELPING HANDS

Many who witnessed it were hoping that they'd never again see a Senate campaign as vile as the 1984 Senate race between the incumbent, Jesse Helms, and his opponent, North Carolina governor Jim Hunt. Those who longed for a return to civility were disappointed, however, at the antics of the Helms crowd in the 1990 reelection campaign against Harvey Gantt, the former mayor of Charlotte.

Although Gantt had an uphill battle against the rural "Jessecrats" who loved their bespectacled hero's right-wing diatribes against the pointy-headed bureaucrats in Washington, the first black U.S. senatorial nominee in North Carolina history somehow managed to take an eight-point lead in the polls three weeks before the election. That's when Helms's diehard backers really went into action. The state's Republican party mailed out 150,000 postcards to residents of heavily black voting areas, warning them that anyone who gave out erroneous information while voting could spend up to five years in prison. Of course, claimed the state GOP, the mailing blitz wasn't intended to keep black voters, who overwhelmingly supported Gantt, away from the polls!

The personally chivalrous but politically strident Helms saved his best stuff for the final ten days of the showdown. Perhaps his telling blow to Gantt was an eleventh-hour television commercial hitting the racially tinged issue of hiring quotas, which was dubbed the "white hands" advertisement. It showed the hands of a white worker crinkling a job application rejection, while the narrator intoned: "You needed that job, but they had to give it to a minority because of a racial quota. Is that really fair?"

Apparently the voters of North Carolina thought not, for Helms was returned to office by 52 to 48 percent, almost the same thin margin of his two previous Senate races.

THE CAJUN CAROUSER

Louisiana governor Edwin Edwards, a ladies' man with a roguish smile and a taste for the good life, usually manages to disarm even his critics with his quick, self-effacing wit. Edwards revels in his reputation as a carouser and even boasted that it contributed to his popularity with Cajun State voters. He once boldly predicted that he would be elected unless he was found in bed with "a dead girl or a live boy."

A stickler for accuracy, however, Edwards advised a reporter covering his 1991 reelection campaign not to believe assertions in a book that he had once slept with six women in one night. The book's author, he explained, "was gone when the last one came in."

THE DUKE'S RUNNING MATE

One candidate's dirty trick is another candidate's effective campaign strategy. There's no doubt, however, that the George Bush team's tactic of "Hortonizing" their Democratic opponent, Massachusetts governor Michael Dukakis, was the most effective political weapon of the 1988 presidential race. The Republicans' relentless, aggressive portrayal of Dukakis as soft on crime, and his failure to rebut the devastating image, severely damaged his chances of occupying the White House.

Like most attacks from the Bush camp, the inspiration originated in the office of Lee Atwater, the vice-president's guitar-strumming young campaign manager, who'd tipped his intentions toward Gov. Dukakis when he said he intended to "rip the bark off the little bastard." True to his word, Atwater assigned a group of researchers, who he referred to as "thirty-five excellent nerds," to probe for weaknesses in Dukakis's record. One of them, Jim Pinkerton, with a helpful tip from White House staffer

Andrew Card, came up with a winner. The nerd patrol discovered that Tennessee senator Al Gore, while running in the Democratic primaries earlier, had blasted Dukakis for giving weekend furloughs to convicted criminals.

One of them had been William "Willie" Robert Horton, Jr., a thirty-seven-year-old felon who'd originally received a lengthy prison sentence for participating in a gas station robbery in which a teenaged attendant had been fatally stabbed a total of nineteen times and stuffed into a garbage can. Years later, after fleeing from a state-sponsored prison furlough program in Massachusetts, Horton had broken into a Maryland home, savagely beating a young auto manager, raping his girlfriend, and ransacking their belongings.

The gleeful Atwater had found his symbol—a violent, menacing albatross to hang around Dukakis's stiff neck. "By the time we're finished, they're going to wonder if Willie Horton is Dukakis's running mate," he boasted. The uneducated Horton, again behind bars, found himself the "star" of nationally televised Republican campaign commercials, and soon received so many media calls that he had to have an adviser screen them. His victims, angered that Dukakis stubbornly refused to apologize for freeing Horton prior to his terrorizing rampage, recorded campaign commercials for Bush. "I'm for Dukakis," said Horton, Prisoner #189182 at the Maryland State Penitentiary, in a comment Bush's handlers gladly labeled an "endorsement."

Democrats railed that publicizing the black Horton's crimes was injecting an ugly racial overtone into presidential politics. But the protests went largely unheeded by voters. At least one of Dukakis's senior staffers blamed the Horton episode for dashing his candidate's chances. "I knew the election was over," said Mark Gearan, Dukakis's deputy press secretary, "when I returned a phone call to a newspaper and I was told the reporter couldn't take my call because she was talking to Willie Horton."

LIST OF SOURCES

SLANDER, LIES, & MUDSLINGING

—Joseph H. Cooper, in *New York Times,* Feb. 21, 1984.

—Peter Hay, *All the President's Ladies: Anecdotes of the Women Behind the Men in the White House* (Viking Press, New York, 1988), p. 108. Paul Boller, in *Presidential Campaigns,* pp. 101–7 (Oxford University Press, New York, 1984). Fawn Brodie, *Thomas Jefferson: An Intimate History* (W. W. Norton & Co., New York, 1974).

—Quoted in Jeff Greenfield, *Playing to Win* (Simon and Schuster, New York, 1980), p. 40.

—Robert Remini, *The Election of Andrew Jackson* (J. B. Lippincott Company, Philadelphia–New York, 1963).

—Donald Cole, *Martin Van Buren and the American Political System* (Princeton University Press, Princeton, N.J., 1984), pp. 264–65. John Niven, *Martin Van Buren and the Romantic Age* (Oxford University Press, New York, 1983), pp. 394–401.

—Paul Boller, Jr., ibid, pp. 84–86; also news clips re: Prof. Clara Rising.

—Ferol Egan, *Frémont: Explorer for a Restless Nation* (Doubleday, New York, 1970).

—Robert W. Johannsen, *Stephen A. Douglas* (Oxford University Press, New York, 1973), pp. 781–86.

—Paul Boller, *Presidential Wives* (Oxford University Press, New York, 1988), pp. 112–13.

—William S. McFeeley, *Grant: A Biography* (W. W. Norton & Co., New York, 1981), p. 282.

—John T. Noonan, *Bribes* (Macmillan Publishing Co., New York, 1984), pp. 462–479.

—Leon Caufield, *The Presidency of Woodrow Wilson* (Fairleigh Dickinson Press, Rutherford, New Jersey, 1966); Edward Weinstein, *Woodrow Wilson: A Medical and Psychological Biography* (Princeton University Press, Princeton, N.J., 1981); Edwin Tribble, *A President in Love: The Courtship Letters* (Houghton-Mifflin, Boston, 1981); Ray Stannard Baker, *Woodrow Wilson: Life and Letters, Volume Four* (Doubleday, Doran and Co., New York, 1931).

—W. A. Swanberg, *Citizen Hearst: A Biography of William Randolph Hearst* (A Scribner Book, Collier Books, Macmillan Publishing Co., New York, 1961), pp. 393–518.

—Bruce Felknor et al. in the Fair Campaign Practices Committee Report (1966), p. 109.

—Ronald Brownstein, *The Power and the Glitter* (Random House, New York, 1991), pp. 40–43. Irving, Amy, and Sylvia Wallace & David Wallechinsky, *The Book of Lists 2*, (A Bantam Book, New York, 1979), pp. 35–36.

—William Safire, *Safire's Political Dictionary* (Random House, New York, 1978), p. 402.

—Franklin Delano Roosevelt, *The Public Papers and Addresses of Franklin D. Roosevelt, 1944–45 Volume: Victory and the Threshold of Peace* (Harper, New York, 1950), p. 290.

—Fawn Brodie, *Richard Nixon: The Shaping of His Character* (W. W. Norton & Co., New York, 1981), p. 306.

—Carl Solberg, *Hubert Humphrey: A Biography* (W. W. Norton & Co., New York, 1984), p. 209.

—Joseph C. Spear, *Presidents and the Press* (MIT Press, Cambridge, MA, 1984), p. 46.

—Barry Goldwater and Jack Casserly, *Goldwater* (Doubleday Publishing, New York, 1988).

—Clark M. Mollenhoff, *Despoilers of Democracy* (Doubleday, New York, 1965), pp. 342–56.

—Jules Witcover, *White Knight: The Rise of Spiro Agnew* (Random House, New York, 1972), pp. 372–95.

—Private files of Jack Anderson, 1531 P Street, N.W., Washington, D.C., *Los Angeles Times* clip files, 1980.

—John Baer, interview, Oct. 8, 1991. Harry Stouffer, interview, Oct. 9, 1991.

—Bates & Associates ad, undated (1990).

—*Vermont Law Review,* (11:33, 1986), as cited by Congressional Research Service report, pp. 37–39. *Chicago Tribune,* Oct. 12, 13, 1984.

—Mark Green with Michael Calabrese, *Who Runs Congress?* (Bantam Books, New York, 1979), p. 214.

—American Association of Political Consultants Code of Ethics, September 4, 1991. Interview with Ralph Murphine of the Murphine Group, Sept. 4, 1991. Interview with Dean Chris Arterton, Sept. 4, 1991.

—Fred Barnes in *The New Republic,* July 27, 1987. Interview with Fred Barnes, Aug. 13, 1991.

—*Time* magazine, Oct. 29, 1990, Nov. 19, 1990. *Washington Post,* Sept. 28, 1991.

—Interview with J. Brian Smith, Aug. 14, 1991. *Campaigns & Elections* magazine, May, 1991, pp. 48–50. *Arizona Republic,* Feb. 9, 1991, p. A10. *Phoenix Gazette,* Feb. 11, 1991, p. A2, *Washington Times,* April 12, 1991. *Roll Call,* Feb. 16, 1991, p. 42.

—*Baltimore Sun*, Sept. 10, 1991.
—Larry Sabato, quoted in *Washington Post*, Nov. 7, 1991.
—*Washington Post*, Nov. 9, 1991, and Nov. 12, 1991. WJLA-TV news report, Nov. 1991.

DIRTY TRICKS

—Tim Coughlin in *Jefferson City (Mo.) Times*, May 31, 1982.
—Denis Lynch, *Boss Tweed: The Story of a Grim Generation* (Boni & Liveright Publishers, New York, 1977), pp. 160–61.
—Stephen Sears, *George B. McClellan: The Young Napoleon*, (Ticknor and Fields, New York, 1988), pp. 372–85.
—Drew Pearson, *The Washington Merry-Go-Round*, Sept. 15, 1936.
—Michael Beschloss, *The Crisis Years: Kennedy and Khruschev, 1960–1963*, (Edward Burlingame Books, Harper/Collins Publishers, New York, 1991), pp. 187–88.
—Bruce Felknor, Fair Campaign Practices Report, 1966.
—Dennis Wainstock, *The Turning Point The 1968 United States Presidential Campaign* (McFarland and Co. Publishers, Jefferson, North Carolina, 1988), p. 169. The *New York Times*, McGeorge Bundy letter to the editor, June 13, 1991.
—Mike Royko, *Boss: Richard J. Daley of Chicago* (E. P. Dutton, New York, 1971), pp. 88–90.
—The Nixon Presidential Archives, Alexandria, Virginia.
—Jeb Magruder, *An American Life: One Man's Road to Watergate,* (Athᴇ.?eum Press, New York, 1974), pp. 167, 202.
—Stephen Ambrose, *Nixon: The Education of a Politician, 1913–1962* (A Touchstone Book, Simon & Schuster, New York, 1987), p. 640. *Regardie's* magazine, Sept. 1989, p. 157. John Erhlichman, *Witness to Power* (Simon & Schuster, New York, 1982), p. 378. Barry Goldwater and Jack Casserly, *Goldwater*, ibid., p. 207. Jeff Greenfield, *Playing to Win*, ibid., p. 217. Bruce Felknor, *Dirty Politics*—Report of the Fair Campaign Practices Committee, 1966, p. 146.
—Charles Colson, *Born Again* (Chosen Books, Old Tappan, N.J., 1976), pp. 70–71. Herbert G. Klein, *Making It Perfectly Clear* (Doubleday & Co., New York, 1980), p. 281.
—*Washington Post*, May 7, 1991.
—Magruder, ibid. p. 177–79. John Dean, *Blind Ambition*, (Simon & Schuster, New York, 1976), pp. 72–79.
—Myra McPherson, *The Power Lovers* (G. P. Putnam's Sons, New York, 1975), pp. 211–13.
—Testimony of Patrick J. Buchanan, Senate Watergate Hearings, Sept. 26, 1973.

—Larry J. Sabato, *The Rise of Political Consultants* (Basic Books, New York, 1981), pp. 164–65.

—Weekly special syndicated column of Jack Anderson and Joseph C. Spear: Nov. 10, 1980. (United Features Syndicate).

—*"Frontline"* public television documentary, April 16, 1991. *"The MacNeil-Lehrer NewsHour"*, June 13, 1991. The Fund For New Priorities, press conference, C-Span network, June 16, 1991. *"Nightline"*, ABC News broadcast. *New York Times, Washington Post, Washington Times, Newsweek* magazine, April–Dec. 1991.

—*Unauthorized Transfers of Nonpublic Information During the 1980 Election: A Report of the Subcommittee on Human Resources, Committee on Post Office and Civil Service,* May 17, 1984.

—Paul Kleppner, *Chicago Divided: The Making of a Black Mayor* (Illinois University Press, Dekalb, IL, 1985), pp. 213, 232.

—Interview with Dan Stanford, Sept. 3, 1991. *Los Angeles Times,* March 3, 1985, p. 28. *San Diego Tribune,* March 1, 1985. *San Diego Union,* March 3, 1985. *San Francisco Chronicle,* March 7, 1991. *Sacramento Bee,* March 10, 1985. *San Francisco Examiner-Chronicle,* March 10, 1985. *Los Angeles Herald Examiner,* March 10, 1985.

—Frank Lutz, *Candidates, Consultants, and Campaigns: The Style and Substance of American Electioneering* (Basil Blackwell, Inc., New York, 1988), p. 21.

—Jack Germond and Jules Witcover, *Blue Smoke And Mirrors* (Viking Press, New York, 1981), pp. 125–31. Peter Goldman and Tonu Fuller, *The Quest for the Presidency, 1988* (A *Newsweek* book, New York, 1989), p. 85.

—*Washington Post,* April 19, 1991.

BRIBERY, BLACKMAIL & OUTRIGHT THEFT

—Irving and Amy Wallace, David Wallechinsky, *Significa,* cited in *Parade* magazine, Nov. 29, 1981, p. 17.

—Matthew Josephson, *The Politicos, 1865–1896* (Harcourt, Brace and Co., New York, 1938), p. 438.

—Nathan Miller, *The Founding Finaglers* (David McKay, New York, 1976), pp. 207–11.

—Josephson, ibid., pp. 93–99, Miller, ibid. pp. 283–86.

—LeRoy Ashby, *William Jennings Bryan: Champion of Democracy* (Twayne Publishers, G. K. Hall, Boston, 1987), pp. 50–71. Dr. Charles McDaniel Rosser, *The Crusading Commoner: A Closeup of William Jennings Bryan and His Times* (Mathias, Van Norty & Co., Dallas, 1937), p. 71. Robert and Leona Train Rienow, *Snuff, Sin & the Senate* (Follett Publishing Company, New York, 1965), pp. 144–47.

—Alfred Steinberg, *The Bosses* (Macmillan Company, New York, 1972), pp. 140–49.

—Michael Dorman, *Dirty Politics from 1776 to Watergate* (Delacorte Press, New York, 1979), pp. 32–33.

—Josephson, Ibid., pp. 512–517.

—Gordon S. Word, *"Politics Without Party,"* The New York Times *Review of Books,* Oct. 10, 1984, p. 20.

—John T. Noonan, *Bribes* (Macmillan Publishing Co., New York, 1984), p. 625.

—Lincoln Steffens, *The Autobiography of Lincoln Steffens* (Harcourt, Brace, New York, 1931), p. 596.

—Bill & Lori Granger, *Lords of the Last Machine: The Story of Politics in Chicago* (Random House, New York, 1987), pp. 31–33.

—Charles Mee, *The Ohio Gang: The World of Warren Harding* (M. Evans and Co., New York, 1981), p. 100.

—Keith Seward, *The Legend of Henry Ford* (Atheneum Press, New York, 1972), pp. 125–31.

—Andrew B. Callow, Jr., *The City Boss in America: An Interpretive Reader* (Oxford University Press, New York, 1976), p. 147.

—R. T. C. Butow and Marc Weiss, *American Heritage* magazine, (Feb./March, 1982). *Washington Post,* Jan. 14, 1982.

—Robert A. Caro, *Means of Ascent: The Years of Lyndon Johnson* (Alfred A. Knopf, New York, 1990), pp. 209–350.

—Tom Wicker, *One of us: Richard Nixon and the American Dream* (Random House, New York, 1991), pp. 256–57. *Washington Times,* Oct. 7, 1991.

—William Miller and Frances Spatz Leighton, *"Fishbait": The Memoirs of a Congressional Doorkeeper* (Prentice-Hall Publishers, Englewood Cliffs, N.J., 1977), p. 21.

—Thomas P. O'Neill and William Novak, *Man of the House: The Life and Political Memoirs of House Speaker Tip O'Neill* (Random House, New York, 1987), pp. 237–39.

—Mark Green with Michael Calabrese, *Who Runs Congress?* (Bantam Books, New York, 1979), pp. 182–83.

—Transcript of news story on WUSA, Channel 9 (Gannett, Washington, D.C.), May 1989: interview with reporter Mark Feldstein, May 29, 1991. *Washington Post,* March 13–19, 1983.

—Sam Smith, *The Progressive,* September 1991; *Rapid City Journal,* Sept. 25, 1991; Sioux Falls *Argus Leader,* Sept., 1991. Press release of Rep. Tim Johnson (D-At Large), Sept. 24, 1991.

—*Wall Street Journal,* Sept. 6, 1991; *New York Times,* Oct. 16, Oct. 31, and Nov. 10, 1991; *Washington Post,* Sept. 27, Oct. 25, Nov. 3, Nov. 9, 1991.

—Kevin Chaffee, Center for Public Integrity report, "Saving For A Rainy Day," Washington, D.C., March 1991; *New York Times,* March 29, 1991; *Wall Street Journal,* March 28, 1991.

SMOKE-FILLED ROOMS

—*Washington Post,* Sept. 22, 1991.

—Robert Remini, *The Election of Andrew Jackson* (J. B. Lippincott Company, Philadelphia–New York, 1963); John T. Noonan, Jr., *Bribes* (Macmillan Publishing, New York, 1984), pp. 449–51.

—Freeman Cleaves, *Old Tippecanoe: William H. Harrison and His Times* (Charles Scribner's Sons, New York, 1939).

—Mark Green and Michael Calbrese, *Who Runs Congress?* (Bantam Books, New York, 1979), p. 266.

—Stephen B. Oates, *With Malice Toward None: The Life of Abraham Lincoln* (Mentor, The New American Library, New York and Ontario, 1977), pp. 191–94, 203.

—Glyndon G. Van Deusen, *Horace Greeley: Nineteenth Century Crusader* (University of Pennsylvania Press, 1953), pp. 400–425. Henry Luther Stoddard, *Horace Greeley: Printer, Editor, Crusader* (G. P. Putnam's Sons, New York, 1946), pp. 304–22.

—Alexander Callow, Jr., *The Tweed Ring* (Oxford University Press, New York, 1975 reprint), pp. 212–13.

—*The Hayes-Tilden Disputed Election of 1876* (Russell and Russell, Atheneum House, 1966 reprint—orig. published in 1906), pp. 45–342. Bernard A. Weisberger, "The Stolen Election," *American Heritage* magazine, July/August, 1990, pp. 18–20.

—Grover Cleveland, quoted in *If Elected . . . Unsuccessful Candidates for the Presidency* by the staff of the Historian's Office, National Portrait Gallery, Smithsonian Institution Press, Washington, D.C., 1972, p. 295.

—William Safire, *Safire's Political Dictionary* (Random House, New York, 1978), p. 93.

—Charles Mee, Jr., *The Ohio Gang: The World of Warren Harding* (M. Evans and Co., New York, 1981), pp. 85–99.

—T. Harry Williams, *Huey Long* (Vintage Books, New York, 1981), p. 181.

—William Miller and Frances Spatz Leighton, *"Fishbait": The Memoirs of the Congressional Doorkeeper* (Prentice Hall Publishers, Englewood Cliffs, N.J., 1977), p. 211. *New York Times,* May 21, 1991.

—Burdett Loomis, *The New American Politician: Ambition, Entrepreneurship, and the Changing Face of Political Life* (Basic Books, New York, 1990), p. 229.

—Minutes of the National Republican Congressional Committee, 1984. Interview with former congressman Tony Coelho, Sept. 9, 1991. Interviews with Coelho, Democratic House aides, Sept. 1991.

THE FINE ART OF SELF-DESTRUCTION

—Sol Barzman, *Madmen and Geniuses: The Vice Presidents of the United States* (Follett Publishing, Chicago, 1974), pp. 48–50.

—Noel Busch, *T.R.: The Story of Theodore Roosevelt and His Influence on Our Times* (Reynal and Company, New York, 1963), pp. 246–77. Paola E. Coletta, *The Presidency of William Howard Taft* (The University of Kansas Press, Lawrence, 1973), pp. 217–47.

—Clark Mollenhoff, *Despoilers of Democracy* (Doubleday, Garden City, New York, 1965), pp. 342–49.

—Adam C. Powell, *Adam by Adam: The Autobiography of Adam Clayton Powell, Jr.* (The Dial Press, New York, 1971), pp. 210–14. James Haskins, *Adam Clayton Powell: Portrait of a Marching Black* (The Dial Press, New York, 1974), pp. 124–44.

—Peter Collier and David Horowitz, *The Rockefellers* (Holt, Rinehardt and Winston, New York, 1976), p. 358.

—Tom Wicker, *One of Us* (Random House, New York, 1991), pp. 296–98.

—Nixon Presidential Archives, Alexandria, Virginia.

—Christopher Matthews, *Hardball* (Summit Books, New York, 1988.

—Stephen Ambrose, *Nixon: The Triumph of a Politician, 1962–1972* (Simon and Schuster, New York, 1989), pp. 505–9, 569–70. *Watergate and the White House, June 1972–July 1973, Volume 1* (Facts On File, New York, 1973, editor, Edward W. Knappman), pp. 71–72.

—Myra McPherson, *The Power Lovers* (G. P. Putnam's Sons, New York, 1975), pp. 232–44.

—Seth Kantor in *Detroit News,* Oct. 17–Nov. 8, 1976.

—Joseph R. Daughen and Peter Binzen, *The Cop Who Would Be King: The Honorable Frank Rizzo* (Little, Brown, Boston, 1977), *Philadelphia Bulletin,* Oct. 29, 1975. *New York Times,* July 7, 1991.

—Jack Germond and Jules Witcover, *Blue Smoke and Mirrors* (The Viking Press, New York, 1981), pp. 69–70.

—*Report of the Special Counsel to the House Committee on Standards of Official Conduct on the Inquiry Under House Resolution 12, 98th Congress, 1st Session, into Certain Narcotics Investigations by the United States Capitol Police,* May 18, 1983. *Final Report of the Special Counsel to the Committee on Standards of Official Conduct on the Investigation into Allegations of Illicit Use of Distribution of Drugs Under House Resolution 518, 97th Congress, and House Resolution 12, 98th Congress,* November 17, 1983. Also, author's private files.

—Montague Kern, *Thirty-Second Politics: Political Advertising in the Eighties* (Praeger Books, New York, 1989), pp. 180–210.

—Roger Simon, *Roadshow* (Farrar, Straus & Giroux, New York, 1990), pp. 55–93. Gail Sheehy, *Character: America's Search for Leadership*

206 LIST OF SOURCES

(Bantam Books, 1990), pp. 37–74. *New York Times Magazine,* May 1988.
—Christine Black and Thomas Oliphant, *All by Myself: The Unmaking of a Presidential Campaign* (The Globe Pequote Press, Chester, Connecticut, 1989), pp. 60–72, 196–97.
—Thomas H. Landess and Richard M. Quinn, *Jesse Jackson and the Politics of Race* (Jameson Books, Ottawa, IL, 1985), pp. 207–11.
—*Wilmington News Journal,* March 8, 1981. *Penthouse* magazine, Nov. 1988. Interview with Joe Trento. Author's private files on Paula and Hank Parkinson investigations.
—Associated Press, *San Antonio Express-News* clips, Sept.–Nov. 1990.
—*Washington Post, Washington Times, New York Times,* NBC News "Expose," transcripts and news clips, April–Nov. 1991.
—*Washington Post,* Nov. 4, 1991.

RED-BAITING, FLAG-WAVING, DEMAGOGUERY

—Marvin Kitman, *The Making of a President, 1789: The Unauthorized Campaign Biography* (Harper & Row, New York, 1989), p. 248.
—Ishbel Ross, *An American Family: The Tafts 1678–1964* (Greenwood Press, Westport, CN, 1964), p.. 188.
—Matthew Josephson, *The Politicos 1865–1896* (Harcourt, Brace & Co., 1938), pp. 364.
—John Taylor in *New York Times.*
—J. T. Salter (editor), *Public Men in and out of Office* (University of North Carolina Press, Chapel Hill, 1946), pp. 284–85.
—Eugene P. Trani and David L. Wilson, *The Presidency of Warren Harding* (The Regents Press of Kansas, Lawrence, 1977), p. 27. Charles Mee, ibid. p. 44.
—The staff of the Historian's Office, National Portrait Gallery, Smithsonian Institution Press, Washington, D.C., 1972, *If Elected . . . Unsuccessful Candidates for the Presidency,* p. 354.
—Gilbert Nations, *The Political Career of Alfred E. Smith,* pp. 55–56. Edward A. Moore, *The Presidential Election of 1928,* pp. 46, 130–76.
—Thomas Edsall, *Power and Money: Writing about Politics 1971–1987* (W. W. Norton & Co., New York, 1988), p. 134. *Baltimore Sun,* Sept. 24, 1980.
—Sam Smith, The *Progressive Review,* Sept. 1991. Joseph Daughen and Peter Binzen, *The Cop Who Would Be King: The Honorable Frank Rizzo,* (Little, Brown, Boston, 1977), pp. 122, 171.
—The files of Drew Pearson, 1946–47; also Irving, Amy and Sylvia Wallace and David Wallechinsky, *The Book Of Lists 2* (Bantam Books, New York, 1980), p. 36.

—Robert S. Allen and William V. Shannon, *The Truman Merry-Go-Round* (Vanguard Press, New York, 1950), p. 271.

—Christopher Matthews, *Hardball* (Summit Books, New York, 1988), pp. 118–21.

—Fawn Brodie, *Richard Nixon: The Shaping of His Character* (W. W. Norton, New York, 1981), pp. 170–84, 232–45. Tom Wicker, *One of Us: Richard Nixon and the American Dream* (Random House, New York, 1991), pp. 33–48, 72–79.

—Stephen Ambrose, *Nixon, Volume One: The Education of a Politician, 1913–1962* (A Touchstone Book, Simon & Schuster, New York, 1987), pp. 279–300.

—Myra McPherson, *The Power Lovers* (G. P. Putnam's Sons, New York, 1975), pp. 210–11.

—Robert Griffith, *The Politics of Fear: Joseph McCarthy and the Senate* (The University of Massachusetts Press, Amherst, 1987), pp. 28–29. Madison, Wisconsin, *Capital Times*, Sept. 28, 1951.

—James Reston, Jr., *The Lone Star: The Life of John Connally* (an Edward Burlingame Book, Harper & Row Publishers, New York, 1989), pp. 295–97.

—Steven Brill, *Harper's* magazine, March 1976, pp. 7–88.

—Edward Koch, *Mayor: An Autobiography* (Simon and Schuster, New York, 1984), pp. 34–35.

—Marc Smolonsky, *Congress Probe* newsletter, 1980.

—*Philadelphia Daily News,* June 1, 1984. Interview with Tony Capaccio, journalist, Washington, D.C., May 1991.

—William D. Snider, *Helms & Hunt* (The University of North Carolina Press, Chapel Hill, 1985), pp. 113–205.

—Peter Goldman and Tony Fuller, *The Quest for the Presidency 1984* (A *Newsweek* book, Bantam, New York, 1985), p. 231.

—*Casper Star-Tribune,* April 6–23, 1989. Interview with Jill Alpert, July 8, 1991. Interview with Dick High, Sept. 1991.

—Hedrick Smith, *The Power Game: How Washington Really Works* (Ballantine Books, New York, 1988), pp. 142–43.

—*Time* magazine, Oct. 22, 1990.

—Interview with Professor Julian Kanter, University of Oklahoma, Aug. 28, 1991.

—*Time* magazine, Nov. 19, 1990, p. 43.

—*Washington Post,* June 26, 1991.

—Roger Simon, *Roadshow* (Farrar, Straus & Giroux, New York, 1990), pp. 203–14. Christine Black and Thomas Oliphant, *All by Myself: The Unmaking of a Presidential Campaign* (The Globe Pequot Press, Chester, Connecticut, 1989), pp. 205–27.

BIBLIOGRAPHY

Confessions of a Muckracker, by Jack Anderson with James Boyd Random House, New York, 1979, pp. 148–49.

New York Times, John Taylor, author (date unknown) (editorial on Blaine/Cleveland incident).

American Heritage magazine, March/April 1982 by Prof. R. C. J. Butow (Also recounted in *Washington Post*, *1/14/82*) *FDR tapes*.

Unauthorized Transfers of Nonpublic Information During the 1980 Election: A Report of the Subcommittee on Human Resources, Committee on Post Office and Civil Service—May 17, 1984.

Report of the Congressional Committees Investigating the Iran/Contra Affair (With the Minority View)—Random House, 1988.

Investigation of Alleged Improper Alterations of House Documents: Report of the Committee on Standards of Official Conduct, U.S. House of Representatives, 98th Congress, First Session, Nov. 14, 1983.

The private files of columnists Drew Pearson and Jack Anderson, 1932–92: 1531 P Street, N.W., Washington D.C.

The Presidential Campaign: An Essay by Stephen Hess—The Brookings Institution, Washington, D.C., 1988.

Tippecanoe and Trinkets Too: The Material Culture of Presidential Campaigns 1824–1984 by Roger A. Fisher—University of Illinois Press, Urbana & Chicago, 1988.

The Quest for the Presidency, 1984 by Peter Goldman & Tony Fuller—a *Newsweek* book, Bantam, New York, 1985.

The Making of a President 1789: The Unauthorized Biography by Marvin Kitman, Harper & Row, 1989.

The Quest for the Presidency, 1988 by Peter Goldman, Tom Matthews and the election team of *Newsweek*. Touchstone, Simon & Schuster, New York, 1989.

Presidential Campaigns by Paul F. Boller, Jr., Oxford University Press, New York, 1984.

The Power Game: How Washington Really Works by Hedrick Smith, Ballantine Books, New York, 1988.

Means of Ascent: The Years of Lyndon Johnson (Volume II) by Robert A. Caro, Alfred A. Knopf, New York, 1990.

One of Us: Richard Nixon and the American Dream by Tom Wicker, Random House, New York, 1991.

Who Runs Congress? by Mark Green with Michael Calabrese, Bantam Books, New York, 1979.

210   BIBLIOGRAPHY

Bribes by John T. Noonan, Jr., Macmillan Publishing Co., New York, 1984.

Candidates, Consultants & Campaigns: The Style and Substance of American Electioneering by Frank I. Luntz, Basil Blackwell, Inc., New York, 1988.

The Rise of Political Consultants; New Ways of Winning Elections by Larry J. Sabato, Basic Books, New York, 1981.

The Election of Andrew Jackson by Robert Remini, J. B. Lippincott Company, Philadelphia–New York, 1963.

Presidential Campaigns by Paul F. Boller, Jr., Oxford University Press, New York, 1984.

The Power Lovers by Myra MacPherson, G. P. Putnam's & Sons, New York, 1975.

Hardball by Christopher Matthews, Summit Books, New York, 1988.

The Sweetest Little Club in the World: Memoirs of Senate Restaurateur Louis Hurst, as told to Frances Spatz Leighton, Prentice-Hall, Englewood Cliffs, New Jersey, 1980.

The Ohio Gang: The World of Warren Harding by Charles L. Mee, Jr., M. Evans & Co., New York, 1981.

Born Again by Charles Colson, Chosen Books, Old Tappan, New Jersey, 1976.

Blind Ambition by John Dean, Simon & Schuster, New York, 1976.

Witness to Power by John Ehrlichman, Simon & Schuster, New York, 1982.

Richard Nixon; The Shaping of His Character by Fawn M. Brodie, W. W. Norton & Co., New York, 1981.

Nixon: Volume I—The Education of a Politician, 1913–1962 by Stephen Ambrose, a Touchstone Book, Simon & Schuster, New York, 1987.

Nixon: Volume II—The Triumph of a Politician 1962–1972 by Stephen Ambrose, Simon & Schuster, New York, 1989.

Watergate and the White House: June 1972–July 1973, Volume I, Facts on File, Inc., New York, 1973.

Washington Expose by Jack Anderson, Public Affairs Press, Washington, D.C., 1967.

Madmen and Geniuses: The Vice Presidents of the United States by Sol Barzman, Follett Publishing Co., Chicago, 1974.

Goldwater by Barry Goldwater with Jack Casserly, Doubleday Publishing, New York, 1988.

Presidential Wives by Paul F. Boller, Jr., Oxford University Press, New York, 1988.

All the Presidents' Ladies; Anecdotes of the Women Behind the Men in the White House by Peter Hay, Viking Press, New York, 1988.

Helms & Hunt by William D. Snider, The University of North Carolina Press, Chapel Hill, N.C., 1985.

Election Journal: Political Events of 1987–1988 by Elizabeth Drew, William Morrow & Co., New York, 1989.

All by Myself: The Unmaking of a Presidential Campaign by Christine Black and Thomas Oliphant, The Globe Pequot Press, Chester, Connecticut, 1989.

Roadshow by Roger Simon, Farrar, Straus & Giroux, New York, 1990.

The Presidents and the Press: The Nixon Legacy by Joseph C. Spear, MIT Press, Cambridge, MA, 1984.

The Hayes-Tilden Disputed Presidential Election of 1876 by Paul Leland Haworth, Russell & Russell (Anheneum House), 1966 (Originally printed in 1906).

Chicago Divided: The Making of a Black Mayor by Paul Kleppner, Northern Illinois University Press, Dekalb, IL, 1985.

Playing to Win: An Insider's Guide to Politics by Jeff Greenfield, Simon & Schuster, New York, 1980.

Boss: Richard J. Daley of Chicago by Mike Royko, E. P. Dutton, New York, 1971.

The Truman Merry-Go-Round by Robert S. Allen and William V. Shannon, Vanguard Press, New York, 1950.

Presidential Wives: An Anecdotal History by Paul F. Boller, Jr., Oxford University Press, New York, 1988.

Despoilers of Democracy by Clark R. Mollenhoff, Doubleday & Co., Garden City, New York, 1965.

Man of the House: The Life and Memoirs of House Speaker Tip O'Neill with William Novak, Random House, New York, 1987.

The Politicos 1865–1896 by Matthew Josephson, Harcourt, Brace and Co., New York, 1938.

Lords of the Last Machine: The Story of Politics in Chicago by Bill & Lori Granger, Random House, New York, 1987.

The Legend of Henry Ford by Keith Seward, Atheneum Press, New York, 1972.

The Presidency of Warren Harding by Eugene P. Trani and David L. Wilson, The Regents Press of Kansas, Lawrence, KN, 1977.

Old Tippecanoe by Freeman Cleaves, Charles Scribner's Sons, New York, 1939.

Fremont: Explorer for a Restless Nation by Ferol Egan, Doubleday, New York, 1977.

With Malice Toward None: The Life of Abraham Lincoln by Stephen B. Oates, Mentor (*New American Library*), New York and Ontario, 1977.

Horace Greeley: Printer, Editor, Crusader by Henry Luther Stoddard, G. P. Putnam's Sons, New York, 1946.

Horace Greeley: Nineteenth Century Crusader by Glyndon G. Van Deusen, University of Pennsylvania Press, Philadelphia, 1953.

Martin Van Buren and the American Political System by Donald B. Cole, Princeton University Press, Princeton, N.J., 1984.

Martin Van Buren: The Romantic Age of American Politics by John Niven, Oxford University Press, New York, 1983.

The Crisis Years: Kennedy and Khrushchev, 1960–1963 by Michael Beschloss, Edward Burlingame Books (Harper/Collins Publishers), New York, 1991.

George B. McClellan: The Young Napoleon by Stephen W. Sears Ticknor & Fields, New York, 1988.

Mayor: An Autobiography by Edward I. Koch, Simon and Schuster, New York, 1984.

Fall from Grace: Sex, Scandal and Corruption in American Politics from 1702 to the Present by Shelley Ross, Ballantine Books, New York, 1988.

Stephen A. Douglas by Robert W. Johannsen, Oxford University Press, New York, 1973.

The Rockefellers by Peter Collier and David Horowitz, Holt, Rinehardt and Winston, New York, 1976.

Huey Long by T. Harry Williams, Vintage Books, New York, 1981.

The Political Career of Alfred E. Smith by Gilbert Owen Nations, the Protestant, Washington, D.C., 1928.

A Catholic Runs for President: The Campaign of 1928 by Edmund A. Moore, P. Smith, Gloucester, Massachusetts, 1968.

William Safire's Political Dictionary by William Safire, Random House, New York, 1978.

An American Life: One Man's Road to Watergate by Jeb Stuart Magruder, Atheneum Press, New York, 1974.

The Wars of Watergate: The Last Crisis of Richard Nixon by Stanley I. Kutler, Alfred A. Knopf, New York, 1990.

Silent Coup: The Removal of a President by Len Colodny & Robert Gettlin, St. Martin's Press, New York, 1991.

The Nixon Presidential Archives, Alexandria, Virginia.

If Elected . . . : Unsuccessful Candidates for the Presidency, 1796–1968 by the staff of the Historian's Office, National Portrait Gallery, Smithsonian Institution Press, Washington, D.C., 1972.

Public Men In and Out of Office—Edited by J. T. Salter, The University of North Carolina Press, Chapel Hill, N.C., 1946.

Mavericks in American Politics: Eight Men Who Forced the Issues of Their Day by Edward N. Kearney, Mimir Publishers, Madison, Wisconsin, 1976.

The Tweed Ring by Alexander B. Callow, Jr., Oxford University Press, New York, 1975. Reprint edition.

"Boss" Tweed: The Story of a Grim Generation by Denis T. Lynch, Boni & Liveright Publishers, New York, 1977.

The City Boss in America: An Interpretive Reader edited with commentary by Alexander B. Callow, Jr., Oxford University Press, New York, 1976.

Time magazine, Oct. 22 & 29; Nov. 19, 1990.

Washington Post: April 16, 1991; April 19, 1991; May 7, 1991; Sept. 27 & 28, 1991.

New York Times: March 29, 1991; May 21, 1991.

Baltimore Sun: Sept. 10, 1991.

Washington Times: April 1, 1991; May 23, 1991.

Casper Star-Tribune: April–Nov. 1990.

Vermont Law Review (11:33), 1986, as cited in *Congressional Research Service Report for Congress: Negative Campaigning: An Overview* by Thomas Neale, Analyst in American National Government, Nov. 2, 1987.

Wall Street Journal: March 28, 1991; Aug. 16, 1991; Sept. 6, 1991.

Detroit News: Oct. 17–29, 1976.

Los Angeles Times: March 3, 1985.

Sacramento Bee: March 10, 1985.

San Diego Union: March 6, 1985.

San Diego Tribune: March 1, 1985.

San Francisco Chronicle: March 7, 1985.

Harper's magazine, "Jimmy Carter's Pathetic Lies" by Steven Brill; March 1976, pp. 77–88.

Penthouse magazine, Nov. 1988.

Regardie's magazine; *"Tuck's Luck"* by Morris Siegel, Nov. 1989, pp. 157–59.

White Knight: The Rise of Spiro Agnew by Jules Witcover, Random House, New York, 1972.

Hubert Humphrey: A Biography by Carl Solberg, W. W. Norton & Co., New York, 1984.

Power and Money: Writing About Politics, 1971–1987 by Thomas Byrne Edsall, W. W. Norton & Company, New York, 1988.

The Lone Star: The Life of John Connally by James Reston, Jr., (Edward Burlingame books), Harper & Row Publishers, New York, 1989.

Grant: A Biography by William S. McFeely, W. W. Norton & Co., New York, 1981.

Thirty-Second Politics: Political Advertising in the Eighties by Montague Kern, Praeger Books, New York, 1989.

An American Life: One Man's Road to Watergate by Jeb Stuart Magruder, Atheneum Press, New York, 1974.

Blue Smoke and Mirrors by Jack W. Germond and Jules Witcover, Viking Press, 1981.

The Power and the Glitter by Ronald Brownstein, Pantheon, 1991.

Despoilers of Democracy by Clark Mollenhoff, Doubleday, Garden City, New York, 1965.

Making It Perfectly Clear by Herbert Klein, Doubleday, Garden City, New York, 1980.

Of Snuff, Sin and the Senate by Robert Rienow and Leona Tran Rienow, Follett Publishing Company, Chicago, 1965.

The Founding Finaglers by Nathan Miller, David McKay publishers.

Citizen Hearst: A Biography of William Randolph Hearst by W. A. Swanberg, A Scribner Book, Collier Books, Macmillan Publishing Company, New York, 1961.

T.R.: The Story of Theodore Roosevelt and His Influence on Our Times by Noel Busch, Reynal and Company, New York, 1963.

The Presidency of William Howard Taft by Paolo E. Coletta, The University Press of Kansas, Lawrence, 1973.

William Jennings Bryan: Champion of Democracy by LeRoy Ashby, Twayne Publishers, a division of G. K. Hall & Co., Boston, 1987.

The Crusading Commoner: A Closeup of William Jennings Bryan and His Times by Dr. Charles McDaniel Rosser: Mathias, Van Norty and Co., Dallas, 1937.

Lincoln the President: Springfield to Bull Run by J. G. Randall, Dodd, Mead & Co., New York, 1956.

The New American Politician: Ambition, Entrepreneurship, and the Changing Face of Political Life by Burdett Loomis, Basic Books, Inc., New York, 1990.

The New York Times Review of Books, "Politics Without Party," by Gordon S. Wood, p. 120, Oct. 10, 1984.

The Turning Point: The 1968 United States Presidential Campaign by Dennis Wainstock, McFarland & Co. Publishers, Jefferson, North Carolina, 1988.

Joe McCarthy and the Press by Edwin R. Bayley, Pantheon Books, New York, 1981.

The Politics of Fear: Joseph R. McCarthy and the Senate by Robert Griffith, The University of Massachusetts Press, Amherst, MA, 1987.

Adam by Adam: The Autobiography of Adam Clayton Powell, Jr., The Dial Press, New York, 1971.

Adam Clayton Powell: Portrait of a Marching Black by James Haskins, The Dial Press, New York, 1974.

Jesse Jackson & the Politics of Race by Thomas H. Landess and Richard M. Quinn, Jameson Books, Ottawa, Illinois, 1985.

The Bosses by Alfred Steinberg, The Macmillan Company, New York, Collier-Macmillan Limited, London, 1972.

Index